Ruth Buxton Sayre

FIRST LADY OF THE FARM

Ruth Buxton Sayre

FIRST LADY OF THE FARM

Julie McDonald

THE IOWA STATE UNIVERSITY PRESS / AMES

To John O. Petersen and Opal Marcussen

WHO KNOW ALL ABOUT COUNTRY LIVING

© 1980 The Iowa State University Press. All rights reserved

Composed and printed by The Iowa State University Press, Ames, Iowa   50010

First edition, 1980

Library of Congress Cataloging in Publication Data

McDonald, Julie,
    Ruth Buxton Sayre, first lady of the farm.

    Includes index.
    1. Sayre, Ruth Buxton, 1896–   2. Farmers' wives—United States—
Biography. I. Title.
HQ1413.S28M23   301.41′0924 [B]   79–17698
ISBN 0–8138–0420–5

FRONTISPIECE: *In 1948 and 1949 Ruth Buxton Sayre was hitting her stride as a globe-trotter, trying to help farm women everywhere.*

CONTENTS

. . . *And with roots so deep*

FOR those of us who have known and worked with Ruth Buxton Sayre, no biography is necessary. She has written her own, as she went; her philosophy is imprinted indelibly on us, her medium. It is a tremendous living "press run"—she has inspired and instructed hundreds of thousands of us stretching from Warren County, the place of her beginnings, literally to the ends of the earth. As the most influential farm woman in the world, her biography is important history. Besides, anyone who has heard one of her wise, charismatic speeches will be reinspired by the Sayre saga, warmly chronicled by Julie McDonald.

To the millions of women striving for equality today, her life is a lesson in "liberation," a pattern for activism. For she was an early activist—a suffragette, marching for women's rights on her college campus. She assumed that she *was* "equal." How could the family farm be anything else than a partnership? Ideas and problems have no gender, she said. Never strident, she was her natural, common-sense self and was accepted with respect in policymaking groups by her male colleagues. But she did her homework and had something to contribute; an independent, careful thinker, she spoke her mind gently but firmly. People listened, because she had the rare gift of vision beyond her time, plus unusual insight into everyday problems.

When she "married the farm," as she says, when she experienced the hardships and deprivations of farm life in the twenties and thirties—that is when she really activated her social concerns for women and the family—at first in her own community, then, in turn, in her county . . . the state . . . the nation . . . the world. She never lost that basic concern for a better life for rural families as she traveled indefatigably throughout the world. She shared her compassion (and hope) with women in the evolving countries of Africa, in the Palestinian refugee camps—wherever she went, her warm personality communicated beyond the barrier of language. She understood. She cared. Women felt her goodwill; she was their friend.

For she had an international mind. Long before it was fashionable, she warned that "a threat to peace and freedom in any part of the world is a threat to peace and freedom in all parts of the world." German farm women never will forget the two months she spent with them in their war-devastated country binding their mental wounds, helping them to reestablish their organization and contact with the world they could not, by themselves, look in the eye.

The word "together" had special meaning for her. She believed in the power of organizations, of working together to get things done. This was her rallying message, from her early days of organizing her neighbors for Iowa State College Extension classes, working her way up through the various levels of the American Farm Bureau Federation's organization of women, becoming its national leader, and through the US Country Women's Council eventually to international presidency of the Associated Country Women of the World.

Through all the honors and acclaim, she remained her unassuming self. She was at home with royalty and villagers alike, but part of her always remained on the family farm in Iowa, which she loved and where she continued to live—alone, after her husband's untimely death. She never lost her commonality, her humility; her feet were firmly on the ground. Down to earth.

Hers has been a leadership of the spirit as well as the mind. A realist, she rallied her fellow workers to accept their role in community and world housekeeping. The roots of war, she said, lie in the human heart. But so do the roots of peace—roots that continue to be cultivated fervently by hundreds of thousands of people for whom Ruth Sayre planted the seeds.

GERTRUDE DIEKEN
Former editor
The Farmer's Wife for *Farm Journal*

BORN a town girl and a banker's daughter, Ruth Buxton Sayre began
her adult life equipped with a degree from a small but prestigious four-
year liberal arts college in a time when women educated beyond high
school were somewhat of a rarity. The only limitation on her future was
the fact that she had majored in German. By the time she received her
diploma from Simpson College, the United States was at war with
Germany, and the use of the German language soon was to be pro-
scribed in Iowa.

Under other circumstances, Ruth Buxton might have found success
in an area traditionally open to women—as a teacher or a professor—
but instead, she followed her heart to the farm, marrying Raymond
Sayre. She respected her husband's deep love of the land homesteaded
by his grandfather, even shared it, but it soon became clear that Ruth
Sayre was a new kind of farm wife. Rather than accept the hardships of
rural life with resignation, she questioned their necessity, not only for
herself, but for all farm women everywhere.

The college girl who marched for the suffragette cause, the student
who learned from a "Socialist" professor that it was not only possible
but often healthy to question the status quo, became the farm wife who
demanded the best for rural people and, more often than not, got it.

From a modest beginning in her own township, she became president of the Associated Women of the American Farm Bureau Federation, stretching the vision of those she met at every level of that
organization. She crossed national boundaries in both body and spirit as
international president of the Associated Country Women of the
World, speaking for more than six million women around the globe.

Known as the "First Lady of the Farm," Ruth Buxton Sayre brought the viewpoint of rural women to the high councils of the land through presidential appointments, often as the only woman in a group of eminent men. There was, however, no tokenism in her appointments. Ruth Sayre was chosen for her abilities, and the late V. B. Hamilton, longtime secretary-treasurer of the Iowa Farm Bureau, said, "When Mrs. Sayre took a position, I never knew a man to oppose her."

How did she command this respect for her opinions? In 1953 she said about her relationship with the all-male Agriculture Advisory Committee under President Dwight D. Eisenhower, "I do not speak until I can make a contribution. I think the cause of women's rights has been hampered when some women fail to follow that rule."

She thought before she spoke, making a careful analysis of the situation, and her remarks were intelligent and sensible. According to those who worked with her through the years, Ruth Sayre had a way of getting straight to the heart of the matter with good humor and without a trace of sentimentality.

A charismatic speaker, she could make her remarks seem like a personal message to each listener, clothing old truths in the shimmer of her own warmth and empathy. Rural women adored her, listened to her, and believed her. She was to them an approachable idol, equally impressive in a huge auditorium or in private conversation.

In what one friend has called "her glory days," the 1940s and early 1950s, Ruth Sayre brought fame to Ackworth, Iowa, a tiny community in Warren County. She grappled with vital human issues—health, schools, safety, international trade, and world peace—and with every victory or advancement, her humility balanced her honors.

Ruth Sayre's influence on the lives of women throughout the world is incalculable, and she is remembered most warmly for bringing out the best in others. Somehow she made them believe they could rise to challenges, and they did, vindicating her belief in the Platonic rule that leaders must pass their torches to others. She said, "A leader stays in office long enough to make her contribution, but not long enough to keep others from making theirs."

Her own remarkable qualities of leadership included a sense of humor, an empathy for the feelings of others, and a delicate sense of timing. As she put it, "You made your appeal from the point of what you thought they would accept." Gradually they were able to accept more, and Ruth Sayre made steady progress without polarization.

Her recurring theme was a plea to farm women to use their heads as well as their hands, to study, to understand, to get out of their kitchens and do some community housekeeping. She also called for the development of the "International Mind" in the interests of world peace, encouraging women to study and grasp political issues formerly left to men.

Liberated long before the word gained its present meaning, Ruth Sayre said, "Women are no dumber than men. They can't be!" She also pointed out, "Farm problems do not have gender. When income is low, the whole family feels the pinch, and when expenses go up, the chicken money and the cream check go for groceries!"

Ruth Buxton Sayre has lived through a great agricultural revolution—from little mechanization of farming methods to total mechanization and from a rural home life of isolation and deprivation to mobility and opportunity for the farm family.

Her own revolution runs parallel to the changes in rural life, and she says, "I wouldn't have missed the chance to live in these times. I guess you would say I am an activist. When something needs doing, I do it instead of just talking about it."

What Ruth Buxton Sayre has done is a matter of record. She has sown the seeds of human betterment, and the harvest is bountiful. Mrs. Sayre's family, friends, associates, and admirers have made the telling of her story possible. Gertrude Dieken, longtime woman's editor of the *Farm Journal,* and Carl Hamilton, vice-president for information and development at Iowa State University, initiated the undertaking, providing every assistance; Mrs. Sayre's son John spent many hours as an expert guide through family memories; and V. B. Hamilton, former secretary-treasurer of the Iowa Farm Bureau, exerted himself mightily in his last illness to testify to the extraordinary qualities of Ruth Buxton Sayre.

Others who helped enormously with facts and anecdotes were Roger Fleming of Albany, New York, former secretary-treasurer of the American Farm Bureau Federation; Alice Van Wert Murray of Ames, Iowa, who has mirrored Mrs. Sayre's interest in national and international organizations for women in agriculture; Louise Rosenfeld, also of Ames, Iowa, now working with International Educational Services at Iowa State University; Laura Lane of Philadelphia, former staff writer for *Country Gentlewoman* and the *Farm Journal,* now engaged in writing, lecturing, and consulting; Grace Cooper Hardy of Duarte, California, Mrs. Sayre's cousin; Mrs. Allan Kline of Des Moines, Iowa, whose late husband was president of the Iowa Farm Bureau and of the American Farm Bureau Federation; and Zoe Kay of Exira, Iowa, a Master Farm Homemaker.

Associated Country Women of the World members who sent help from abroad include three past international presidents: Lady Binney of

England, Gerda Van Beekhoff of the Netherlands, and Aroti Dutt of India. Two English women, Stella Bell, longtime general secretary of ACWW, and Dorothy McGrigor, an enthusiastic member of the international organization, sent recollections of work and friendship with Mrs. Sayre.

Mrs. Sayre's papers are in the Manuscript Collection of the Division of the State Historical Society of Iowa, Iowa City, Iowa, and gratitude is due Peter Harstad, director of the society; Joyce Giaquinta, curator of manuscripts; and Mary Bennett for every assistance and permission to reproduce photographs from the collection.

Many others from town and country helped with the right information at the right moment, and Ruth Buxton Sayre herself bore endless questions graciously, making me welcome in her life. Knowing her has increased an already robust pride in being an Iowa woman.

Ruth Buxton Sayre

FIRST LADY OF THE FARM

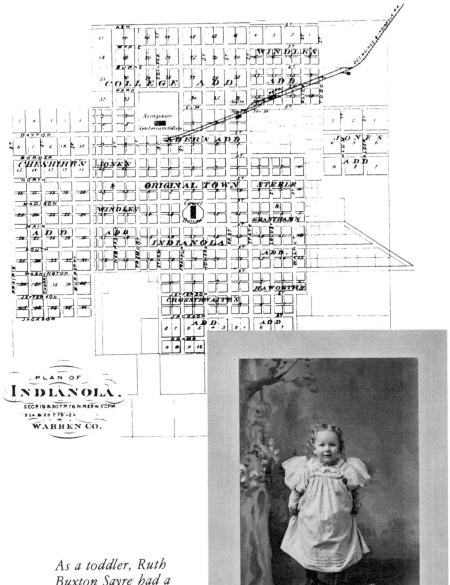

As a toddler, Ruth Buxton Sayre had a china-doll fragility that belied her lively energy.

Strong Stock

RUTH BUXTON SAYRE was born Saturday, January 25, 1896, in Indianola, Iowa, in a little yellow house on West Ashland Street. She was the first child of her young parents, Anna McLaughlin Buxton and William Buxton, Jr., and she said, "I don't think it made any difference that I was a girl."

Her father, reared with four sisters, was not unaccustomed to a household of females, and her mother, an accomplished musician and expert needlewoman, looked forward to passing these arts on to a daughter.

In 1896 life in the 47-year-old Warren County Seat was quiet and intimate. People the Buxtons knew talked about Simpson College, Methodist church affairs, or the businesses around the square, and the Buxton name was prominent in each of these spheres. The birth of a daughter to Anna and William Buxton, Jr., was big news at Sunday morning worship in the First Methodist Episcopal Church of Indianola and on Monday at the Warren County Bank at the corner of Howard and East Salem streets, where the new father was cashier and the grandfather, William Buxton, Sr., was bank president.

The academic community at Simpson College was pleased to hear that the school's benefactor, William Buxton, Sr., had a new grandchild, as were the men at Keeney's Livery, Indianola's "favorite loafing place," where William Buxton, Jr., went to smoke. His wife would not permit this indulgence in the little yellow house.

As soon as Anna Buxton was receiving visitors, her friends and Pi Beta Phi sorority sisters came to admire the baby, and one whose opinion the new mother valued greatly said, "I can tell by looking at her that she'll amount to something."

Anna Buxton believed the prediction because, aside from natural maternal pride, she believed that a great deal could be said for the qualities that little Ruth stood to inherit.

After sampling and rejecting the life of a Manchester factory worker, Ruth's paternal grandfather had left his home in Derbyshire, England, in 1853 to settle in the United States on a claim he had scouted two years earlier in Warren County, Iowa.

On his way to the Middle West, William Buxton, Sr., kept a highly literate travel journal, and an early entry reads, "I think the ladies of Philadelphia surpass anything I ever saw in any other city for beauty and dress."

By December he was nearing his destination, and on Sunday, Christmas Day, 1853, he "walked over to Carlisle twelve miles, which is to be my future home." Buxton settled in, and from then on, the journal entries are laconic, dealing with planting, plowing, and "sundries."

Life at Carlisle was sweeter when Betsy Bramhall accepted Buxton's proposal. A journal entry for April 25, 1858, reads, "Took an important step in life, namely, was married to Miss Betsy Bramhall after nearly a year's faithful courtship and so settled myself down at least for the present. Mr. Burgelt performed the official part of the ceremony at about 4 o'clock p.m. in the presence of a large company of friends and neighbors. The ceremony was short but just as good as if so much longer."

Betsy's illness in September 1859 occasioned the only further mention of her in many journal pages. Buxton wrote, "Betsy taken sick. Had a very hard time. Thought she would have to undergo a surgical operation and sent to the Fort for assistance, Dr. Ward being some scared." The threat passed, and entries for the next two days are identical: "Waiting on the sick."

The Buxtons were members of the first class of the Carlisle Methodist church, but at Christmas they attended Episcopalian services in Des Moines to assuage William's homesickness for the high church ritual of his youth.

For the first ten years of their marriage, the Buxtons lived in a log house on the 400 acres they homesteaded near Carlisle. The Methodist preacher always was welcome in their home, and on two occasions, he brought comfort in bereavement. Betsy Buxton bore seven children, two of whom died in infancy. The survivors were Elizabeth A., Sarah E., William, Jr., Clara, and Agnes.

In 1893 William Buxton sold his Carlisle land, moved to Indianola, and bought a controlling interest in the Warren County State Bank. With a fond backward look at the years of struggle, Betsy Buxton said, "If I were twenty years younger, I would give away all we've got and make it over again."

They moved next door to the Indianola Methodist church, where William Buxton taught a Sunday School class of young women and Betsy was occupied with good works. Her Christian charity extended to taking over the duties of her sick laundress, washing other people's clothes to keep the woman from losing badly needed customers.

The Buxtons were true pioneers, and their legacy to their grand-daughter was self-discipline, a strong sense of duty, stoicism in the face of misfortune, and a belief in the importance of education.

These qualities were matched on the maternal side. Dr. William Reynolds, Anna Buxton's grandfather, was born in Bristol, England. He was a graduate physician with the British army. Posted to Egypt during the Turkish-Egyptian war of the 1830s, Reynolds was captured at Tripoli. Upon his release, he came to the United States, lived briefly in Pennsylvania, and finally settled at Iowa City in a house at the corner of Washington and Gilbert streets. He operated a private school, where Anna Buxton's mother, Jane Anna (Jennie) was a teacher. Dr. Reynolds was the first superintendent of public instruction in the territory which became the state of Iowa.

Claudius B. McLaughlin, Anna Buxton's father, was born in Utica, New York, of Scottish parents who brought him to Davenport, Iowa, in the mid-1850s. Working as a railroad surveyor for the Chicago and Rock Island line between Davenport and Iowa City, young Claudius earned the respect and affection of Ebenezer Cook, a wealthy Davenport land locater and financier.

Claudius McLaughlin and Jennie Reynolds met in Iowa City, where they were married September 8, 1857. Five children were born to them, and three boys died in infancy. The surviving daughters were Anna—Ruth's mother—and Ida.

The warm relationship between the McLaughlins and the Cooks of Davenport continued. The McLaughlins were Episcopalian before they came to Indianola, and Anna cherished a prayer book from her god-mother, Clarissa Cook, a woman of wide philanthropy who endowed a home for elderly women that still bears her name and made substantial contributions to establish the Davenport Public Library. Ebenezer Cook left $5,000 to Claudius McLaughlin in his will.

After serving the Chicago and Rock Island Railroad as a station agent in Iowa City for a number of years, Claudius McLaughlin followed the line west, moving his family to Indianola in 1876. They lived a few blocks southeast of the square, and Jennie McLaughlin opened her home to roomers of refinement such as female members of the Simpson College faculty.

Anna McLaughlin studied music at the Simpson Conservatory, graduating in 1890 with an exhibition of her talents that included singing "I Am Content" by Saintore, playing a violin solo, and performing with a piano quartet.

Among the members of Pi Beta Phi, Anna's sorority, were the Buxton sisters, and she came to know their brother Wil, a quiet and serious Alpha Tau Omega. Soon Anna and Wil were going to chapel together and to sorority and fraternity parties.

After graduating from Simpson, William Buxton, Jr., became president of the bank at Carlisle, which offered more honor than income. Then he bought an interest in a business with his sister Elizabeth's husband, James M. Kittleman, investing in Kittleman and Buxton Clothing and Tailoring on the east side of the Indianola square. In 1892 he took a bookkeeping job at the Warren County Bank.

His marriage to Anna McLaughlin in her parents' home January 3, 1894, was described as "one of the most brilliant weddings that has occurred in our city." Anna wore a gown with short puffed sleeves, ruffles, and a tight midriff fashioned with a point. Dr. Emory Miller, the Methodist minister, performed the ceremony, and an old shoe was suspended in the bay window for luck.

After a honeymoon at the elegant new Ponce de Leon hotel in St. Augustine, Florida, the young couple came home to the little yellow house on West Ashland Street, and the new Mrs. Buxton devoted herself to homemaking, fine needlework, and participation in groups like the Bible Club, the Shakespeare Club (which provided "food for mind and body"), and the Ladies' Aid and Missionary Society at the Methodist church.

The Bible Club consisted of a dozen women who met the second Tuesday of the month at three o'clock for three hours of afternoon study followed by an evening meal shared with husbands and children. After supper, the entire company visited for precisely one hour and parted with the singing of "God Be with You 'til We Meet Again." The club, organized by Mrs. J. B. Gifford in 1887, met twelve months of the year with no vacation, and being the hostess was a monumental undertaking.

The Shakespeare Club, organized the same year, met the third Monday of the month from September to May for the study of literature. The members also enjoyed meals worthy of literary immortality. One menu included blue point oysters on the half shell, bouillon, turkey with oyster dressing, frappe with Neapolitan ice cream and Edam cheese.

The young Buxtons were in comfortable financial circumstances, and in time they would be well-to-do, but Anna had been taught to save, and the ingrained habit would stay with her for life. She practiced industry and admired it where she found it, as in a black Simpson College student named George Washington Carver who transferred to Iowa State College the year after her graduation from the conservatory. In Indianola Carver lived next door to her parents, and he ironed shirts and patched pants for college boys in a woodshed to earn money for his education. Carver created beautiful floral paintings, and Anna remembered the disappointment of Etta M. Budd, director of the Simpson School of Art, when he was lost to art because he grew things even better than he painted them.

The big event of the year for Anna was commencement week at Simpson College. Graduates who lived in Indianola joyously prepared hospitality for returning alumni, and though it was more difficult with a baby to care for, Anna cleaned house furiously for weeks to prepare for guests arriving on the Sunday for the Baccalaureate sermon and vesper service, Alumni Day for class reunions, a grand banquet for members of all classes, a Class Day when Maypoles were wound, and finally, the commencement exercises on Thursday.

This week was a wonderful expression of the warm town and gown relationship in Indianola the year around. Early graduates reminisced about planting the "whispering maples" when Dr. Alexander Burks was college president; the strawberries that grew on the campus along with wildflowers in the 1870s; and "Old Bluebird," the early brick classroom building painted the color of lead. They spoke of the smoky stoves in the early years and admired Ladies' Hall, built in the administration of Dr. Edmund Simpson Holmes when Anna was at the conservatory. Some of the old-timers recalled the days when the college was considered "out of town" and students waded through mud to reach it.

Former classmates of the Buxtons came to the little yellow house to admire the baby Ruth, and as the young parents enjoyed their guests, they felt secure in a happy present and sanguine about the future. They gave little thought to the past of their community, as Indianola was too young to look in any direction but forward, and they would leave delving into history and cherishing antiques to a later generation.

Warren County, where the Buxtons and McLaughlins had put down roots, was one of twelve counties reorganized by one of the last acts of the Territorial Legislature. It was named for General Joseph Warren, the Boston physician and chairman of public safety who sent Paul Revere and William Dawes to warn the citizens before the Battle of Lexington. Warren died at Bunker Hill, long known as "the place where Warren fell."

The city of Indianola was located in June 1849, and while the officials charged with that duty ate a picnic lunch, Sheriff Paris P. Henderson happened to glance at the newspaper wrapped around his food. He read aloud the *New York Sun* account of a load of dromedaries from Smyrna, to be used in the expansion of the American southwest, being landed at a Texas seaport called Indianola.

Alfred D. Jones, the surveyor, suggested that Indianola would be a good name for the new county seat, and the others agreed. The camel venture failed, some of the beasts running wild and others being sold to circuses, and the port of Indianola, Texas, was lost in oblivion, but its namesake flourished in Iowa.

Warren County was in the path of the 1850 gold rush, and the scant population of the new county seat watched the resulting bedlam with amazement. If an ox got sick, forcing its owner to drop out of the westward procession, another wagon filled the gap immediately. Gold fever slacked in June of that year, only to flare again when small particles of impure gold were found in Virginia Township, Warren County.

The first frame house was built in Indianola in 1850, and newcomers lived in a log house just west of what became the Simpson campus until they could build their own homes. The log building was called Naturalization House.

Z. H. Hocket was the first merchant in the business community, and "there was not a single drinking saloon in the place," thanks to the ban on drink by the Methodist church, the first and, for a time, only church in Indianola.

The courthouse was in the center of the public square surrounded by business houses with four or five blocks of private residences in all directions. The square was not paved until 1903, which meant that Claudius McLaughlin picked his way to the Chicago and Rock Island station through quagmire streets spring and fall, and the women of the town walked daintily along board sidewalks. The townspeople spoke of Depot Street, Cemetery Street, and the Square, seldom calling the thoroughfares by their proper names.

The money panic of 1893 prompted William Buxton, Sr., to buy a controlling interest in the Warren County Bank in a three-story building on the south side of the square, and he promoted his son from bookkeeper to cashier, an act of paternal confidence rather than nepotism.

William Buxton, Sr., gave land valued at $50,000 to Simpson College, and he also was part of a stock company to purchase the press and material of the *Independent,* an Indianola newspaper, and establish the *Warren County Leader.* The announcement of the formation of the Indianola Publishing Company for that purpose stated, "It will be radically Republican in politics, striving at all times to maintain the right as God gives us to see the right. It will take an active part in all questions for the advancement of a higher morality. It will always be found upon the side of education and temperance and a warm advocate of all public improvement."

The Indianola Publishing Company's statement of purpose gives an accurate profile of the town's thinking in the late Victorian period, but after about three years, Buxton and his associates "tired of the work of trying to continue a newspaper" and turned their energies elsewhere.

The chief concern of the Buxtons, father and son, was to serve the farmers who made up seventy-five percent of the population of Warren County. Most farmed less than 200 acres with horses and a walking plow and jounced to town over rutted dirt roads in horse-drawn wagons to exchange cream and eggs for flour and sugar. They did not stop to borrow books from the library in a room above the bank presided over by Miss Hannah Babb. After a long day of labor unchanged in its nature in 2,000 years, the farmer and his wife were too exhausted to read by the dim light of a coal oil lamp. Their social life consisted of going to church and visiting with neighbors after the service. Their children attended one-room schools, and few went on to high school. A Simpson College student from the farm was a remarkable rarity.

Anna McLaughlin Buxton worked hard too. She baked, sewed, cleaned, and exercised her mind and talents, but her life as a young matron in the county seat offered more satisfactions and amenities than any farm wife enjoyed.

These circumstances changed very little in the years when Ruth Buxton Sayre was growing up, and in time, the contrast would strike her forcibly. Rather than accept existing conditions with stoic resignation, she would try to change them, not only for herself but for others.

2

The Formative Years

RUTH BUXTON was a beautiful child with blonde curls and blue eyes, and she said, "Mother always was having my picture taken." Except in a pose kneeling barefoot in a soulful prayer, the little girl faces the lens head-on, eyes alight with abundant energy. In another pose, she lifts her skirt daintily as if to dance.

Anna Buxton taught her pretty child a little dance, neglecting to make it clear to Ruth that performances were strictly for a home audience. Ruth danced for the ladies at a church Circle meeting, embarrassing her mother and Grandma Buxton. Dancing was not quite Methodist, it seemed, and Ruth never indulged in it in later years, though her childen would.

The blonde, photogenic curls were a trial to Ruth when they had to be brushed over her mother's finger. One day the iceman arrived during a hair-brushing session and said, "Will you give me a curl?" Before Anna Buxton realized what was happening, Ruth had snatched up scissors and whacked off a curl from the middle of her forehead. The iceman was abashed, Mrs. Buxton was devastated, and Ruth, direct as she would always be, was puzzled because she thought she had done what was wanted.

Even as a child, Ruth Buxton understood power. She knew that her father had it, and yet she was willing to challenge him by locking him in the woodhouse. She said simply, "When he hollered for help, I walked away." For a moment, small as she was, she had some power of her own, and she liked the feeling.

Anna Buxton had some power too. Ruth liked to roam, and even in a small, quiet town like Indianola, her mother was afraid to indulge the child's gypsy tendencies. When reasoning, scolding, and spanking (the latter by her father because her mother was too tenderhearted to spank) failed to keep Ruth in her own yard, Anna Buxton tied her to a tree with a rope. A Simpson student of that day has written, "I remember seeing you tied to a tree so you couldn't run away." Where did Ruth want to go? "I wanted to go if there was any place at all to go," she said.

She might have run away with the gypsies who came to Indianola in covered wagons at county fair time, but their appearance and way of life was so different that she was afraid. She said, "I wanted to see them, but I was scared to death, so I just peeked out from the front porch."

A difference that made no difference to Ruth was color. Sam White, a black janitor at the church, and his wife Cindy, who "helped

[LEFT] *The belle of the neighborhood at three, Ruth was looking for new worlds to conquer.*

Ruth's fluffy bangs looked grand with her Sunday finery, even if they were *an accident.*

out when people had company'' lived near the Buxtons, and Ruth played happily with their children.

Another neighbor child caused Ruth some grief. Ilo Browne, who later married Henry A. Wallace, practiced the piano diligently and played well, inspiring Anna Buxton's praise and the comment to Ruth, "If you would practice the way she does, you could play as well!'' Ruth responded with a fervent wish that Ilo would move away.

Just after the turn of the century, William Buxton, Jr., decided to build a new home for his wife and child and contracted for the construction of an imposing house with a Victorian cupola and wide porches at 500 East Salem Street. While the house was being built, Ruth climbed a two-story ladder to the top of the cupola and refused to come down, terrifying her mother. They moved into the house when Ruth was five.

Anna Buxton's older sister Ida lived a block to the west, and Ruth could go to her house safely or walk to a pear tree two blocks west when it was time for her father to leave the bank so she could "ride'' home in his arms.

The Scroggs family with a houseful of children lived across the street, which saved Ruth from the loneliness of an only child, and in any case, her days as such were numbered. A sister, Alice Margaret, was born when Ruth was six, and she said, "I can't remember feeling left out.'' Because of Ruth's difficult birth, the Buxtons had postponed enlarging their family, but the advent of Alice was less painful, and the interval would shorten thereafter. The big house on East Salem Street had room for more.

Ruth was busy adjusting to Hawthorne School, a big, brick building that might have seemed formidable had it not been just two blocks from Grandma McLaughlin's house, where there was love, food, and boxes of stereopticon slides.

"I liked school,'' Mrs. Sayre recalled, "but I don't think I was too good in deportment.''

Grandma Buxton was not well, but with the help of a housekeeper named Lily, she carried on as if she were. She died in 1901, and one of the last acts of her life was to wash and re-lay the padding for the altar carpet in the Methodist church. Her death was the first that Ruth Sayre remembered. "Father came home and said, 'My mother is gone.' I had never heard his voice sound so hollow and hopeless. Mostly, the men die early, but in this case, it was the other way around.''

William Buxton, Sr., was lonely without Betsy, his log cabin bride, and in 1902 he remarried. The second Mrs. Buxton was Frances Carpenter, the widow of a Simpson faculty member, who had come to live with her daughter and son-in-law, the Harry Hoppers. The Buxton and Hopper houses faced each other across the street, and both William

*Spacious and handsome, the new home at
500 E. Salem Street showed the rising fortunes
of the Buxtons.*

Buxton, Sr., and Frances Carpenter spent a good deal of time sitting on
their respective front porches. Inevitably, they looked at each other, and
one thing led to another. The match was not regarded with much enthusiasm by the Buxton family, but, Mrs. Sayre said, "It was a good
arrangement for him."

Life went on much as it had before in those Edwardian years that
now seem golden: family dinners on Sunday with five chickens fried on
a coal stove and a gallon freezer of cream cranked in chips of winter
from the icehouse until it was time to enjoy the cold treat. Table talk
was about farming, church, and business, and no Buxton was permitted
to "enjoy" ill health. Aches and pains were concealed like a guilty
secret. Ruth knew about her mother's frequent headaches, however.
She said, "I would come home and find her with a big shawl over her
head."

When the family gathered at the East Salem Street house for
Sunday dinner, William Buxton, Jr., might excuse himself after the
meal to read the London *Times,* and the children were to read quietly or
look at stereopticon slides. Ruth also enjoyed watching the world shrink
or expand, depending on which end of her father's binoculars she put

to her eye. Sunday blue laws were very much in effect. An alternative to quiet home pursuits was hitching an old white horse named Nell to the surrey and riding out into the country to visit a farm in which Father had an interest.

"I always hoped the farm wife would serve cake," Mrs. Sayre said, confessing that she did not have the remotest notion that she would someday be a farm wife herself.

Ruth's mother read to her constantly, and as soon as she could read for herself, she began to haunt the free circulating library, where Miss Hannah Babb now was assisted by Miss Maude Fenner. Armed with a reading list prepared by Anna Buxton, Ruth searched the shelves, greeting friends in a brief whisper to avoid Miss Babb's shushing. There was talk of a new library to be built with money from Andrew Carnegie.

Christmas was the only time when Ruth Buxton's love for books ebbed. In the magic excitement of Christmas Eve at the church with Santa Claus and a beautiful tree, Ruth squirmed, overheated in a wool dress over long underwear, and hoped against hope that she would find a doll in her Christmas stocking. All the other girls would get dolls, but Ruth would receive books like *Captain January* or *Little Women*. Books were fine most of the time, but not at Christmas.

As a member of the Shakespeare Club, Anna Buxton subscribed to a travel magazine, and Ruth read it avidly, longing to see the faraway places described. When her mother told her to turn out the lights and go to sleep, Ruth would steal a few more paragraphs by leaning out of her room to read by the dim light in the hall.

When Ruth was eight, her sister Martha was born, and now she could be trusted to watch Alice and the new baby for brief intervals. She said, "I didn't like being the baby-sitter! I wanted to go!" However, when she was forced to stay at home, she did not lack for amusement. At an earlier age, she had paraded down the street nude except for a pink parasol when her mother went out for the milk, but now she made a dash for her mother's wardrobe to try on the ruffled rose silk dress she loved best, parading before a pier mirror in sheer ecstasy.

On one occasion she had dressed up in her mother's clothes and walked to the bank, thinking her father would be charmed by her appearance. He was nothing of the sort, and without a word, he snatched her hand to walk her home.

Ruth was good at make-believe. The first landing of the open stairway in the Salem Street house made an excellent stage when she could round up the Scroggs children and other neighbors to put on a play. Her golden curls made her the only possible choice for the heroine in any drama, and after seeing the Ringling Brothers Circus, she was bent on being a circus bareback rider in spangles.

Family travel gave Ruth a taste for new experiences and friendships, as this 1903 pose with a Colorado burro attests.

Anna Buxton and her daughters enjoyed sea bathing near Long Beach, California, in the winter of 1906.

The Indianola Chautauqua was organized in 1905, and the Buxtons went to the big tent seating 3,000 on the Simpson College ball park to hear speakers like Booker T. Washington and Billy Sunday.

That year was memorable in many ways. In September lightning struck the chicken exhibit tent at the Warren County Fair, killing four men, seriously injuring seven, and inflicting stunning shocks on others in the vicinity. This may have been Ruth's first acquaintance with natural disaster.

Her grandfather retired from the bank in 1905, and as he settled his business affairs, he made arrangements to give the city of Indianola a $5,000 tract of land to be developed into a park by Dr. John L. Tilton, a Simpson College geology professor. The actual date of the gift was February 17, 1906, and in time, the park would have gates and a gazebo and would be used by the college as a nature study site.

Even before his retirement, William Buxton, Sr., and his wife had been wintering in California, and they had made three trips to Europe and visited his boyhood home in England. All the Buxtons liked to travel. A family album photograph shows Ruth hugging a burro in Colorado in 1903, and she said, "I remember going to Texas or California in the winter."

William Buxton, Jr., took his family and "a girl to help" west in the winter of 1906, and Ruth was enrolled in school at Long Beach. A photograph of Ruth and her mother wading in the Pacific in ruffled bathing dresses and long stockings epitomizes the modesty of the period, and soon Anna would abandon the beach because of pregnancy. Mrs. Sayre said, "My brother Bill was born during the San Francisco earthquake, but in Long Beach."

The family stayed in Iowa the following winter, and William Buxton, Jr., was in Mexico with Harry Hopper inspecting land for investment in February 1907 when Anna called him home. Their second daughter, Alice Margaret, had contracted cerebral meningitis and was suffering intensely. Buxton arrived in time to see his five-year-old daughter before she died at 7 a.m., Tuesday, February 11, and funeral services were held in the East Salem Street house at 10 a.m. on Valentine's Day.

Ruth was 11, Martha was three, and Bill was still a baby when their mother was engulfed by this bereavement, and Ruth Sayre said, "Mother was in deep mourning for months." During this period, Ruth sometimes would stay overnight with her McLaughlin grandparents, sleeping on a folding cot they kept in the closet for her. She said, "They called the pantry 'the buttery,' and there was always something good in it."

Through the years Grandma McLaughlin had grown deaf, and Mrs. Sayre said, "Grandpa kept house, and Grandma sat in a wicker chair with her horn." The McLaughlins celebrated their golden wedding anniversary with a grand reception at Aunt Ida's house September 7, 1907. Ruth, feeling very grown up, helped with the serving.

Ruth Buxton did not learn to manage money at an early age. She said, "We had hired girls from the country who wanted to go to school in Indianola, and they probably weren't paid very much—maybe three dollars a week. I was paid nothing, and no one had heard of allowances. When I did get a nickel, I rushed to Daddy Peck's grocery for six Ferndale chocolates, normally a cent apiece."

Her unpaid labors at home consisted of pitting cherries, washing and drying dishes, setting the table, sweeping the porch, and straightening up and dusting before a new hired girl came, "to be ready for her."

In 1908 the Indianola establishments that might have tempted Ruth Buxton to part with money when she had it included the Lyric

Ruth Buxton's grandfather and father bore the name William, and her brother does also.

Theatre, the Crystal Theatre, Clore's Big Variety Store, Harvey's Department Store, and the Palace Book Store. With plenty of good cooks in the family, she probably had little use for Sprague's and Hoyt's restaurants and Swartslander's cafe.

Walking on the square (now paved), Ruth offered a respectful greeting to Dr. Emory Miller, the Methodist pastor, as he rode past on his black mare, Jane. Ruth had been trained to mind her manners and never felt the sting of the thin willow switch her eighth grade teacher used to maintain order.

"I got good grades in school except when something else was more interesting," Ruth Sayre said, "but I had no feeling for math and would like to have abolished it."

Her young life was filled with study, church, reading for pleasure, and the restored normalcy of home life on East Salem Street. There were aunts to visit—her father's sisters Helen (Ella) Cooper and Clara Nicholson in Des Moines and Elizabeth Kittleman and Agnes Little (always called "Aunt Pet") in Berwyn, Illinois.

Other excitements were a trip to Des Moines with her mother to see Maude Adams in *Peter Pan* and a revival meeting at the Methodist church. When the evangelist issued the altar call, Ruth "came forward" with her friends, shocking her father, who told her dryly that her infant baptism "would suffice."

When she was asked many years later, "Were you always a Methodist?" Mrs. Sayre said with that rich bubble of laughter so characteristic of her, "I never had any choice!"

3

Learning and Loving

AS a high school girl, Ruth Buxton was greatly interested in clothes. Her mother would take her shopping in Des Moines, and she said, "If I liked one dress and she liked another, we'd get the one she liked. And I didn't have a lot to wear. Mother always was saving and never bought anything that wasn't necessary."

Be that as it may, Ruth cherished her high school wardrobe enough to keep a scrapbook of fabric swatches and sketches of the clothes. Beside the drawing of a blue messaline gown is the note, "The one and only school dress. I wore a white jabot at the neck when I could find a decent one." Labeled "One of my old standbys" is a blue and gold print trimmed with blue messaline, and the "Sunday-go-to-church" gown was navy velvet with gold and coral bead trim, worn with a white beaver hat. Messaline must have been *the* fabric (lightweight and silky with high lustre), as Ruth's senior reception gown was sky blue chiffon over blue messaline. Another favorite dress was white embroidered voile with lace inserts.

When Ruth began to date, she was escorted to school and church functions by Howard Smith, son of the Indianola superintendent of schools, but she was very much aware of a boy from New Virginia who rented a room in Indianola where he would live while attending high school until his parents, Will and Mamie Sayre, bought land across from the cemetery south of town. Raymond Sayre's grandfather, Enoch S. Sayre, came from the Old Dominion by wagon to settle near New Virginia, and Raymond was bent on going back to farm the family land when he had completed his education.

"I thought he was real nice because he was a football player," Mrs. Sayre said with a chuckle. "He was a church goer, worked with the YMCA in high school, and was a nice fellow all around. His family was nice too, but they were farmers."

Close acquaintance between the two was not immediate. Ruth was occupied with Howard Smith, occasionally going out with Louis Pendry, who lived across the street, and Raymond Sayre was interested in a girl named Mary Sampson.

Ruth had other interests too. She won a creative writing prize for a Christmas story and made her first public speech to a high school Girl Reserve group. Once the speech was over, she realized she had enjoyed it, and, as she followed the political campaigns of Theodore Roosevelt and later Woodrow Wilson, she analyzed the oratory with interest. A good speech, she decided, was a mixture of facts and emotion.

This 1900 photograph of Raymond Sayre with his parents, Will and Mamie, shows an earnestness later tempered by good humor.

By now the Buxtons owned an automobile, a Model T Ford that replaced Old Nell for Sunday rides in the country. Ruth Sayre's cousin, Grace Cooper Hardy, recalls, "Old Nell never blinked an eyelid when an agent brought the first automobile to Indianola for a demonstration."

Ruth was eager to learn to drive, but she assumed (correctly, no doubt) that her father would be against the idea. "He was always very conservative," she said.

One Sunday morning Ruth managed to stay home from church, and when her parents were safely singing the Doxology, she cranked up the Ford, did everything she had watched her father do, and backed the car out between the two posts that bordered the East Salem Street drive. Stopping the car in front of the Scroggs residence, she honked and invited three or four of the Scroggs brood to go for a ride. Her self-confidence precluded any concern about involving them in an accident.

Exhilarated by her newfound skill and the admiration of her young passengers, Ruth drove the Ford several miles east of Indianola. This took longer than she expected, and on the return trip she was horrified to see Methodists strolling home from church. She arrived at the Buxton driveway just as her parents approached the house, and the sight of her father watching silently with folded arms so unnerved her that, she said, "I couldn't get between the two posts. I heard about that quite a bit!" But she knew how to drive, having tackled the learning in her usual manner, head-on.

When Ruth's cousin, Raymond Cooper, was graduated from Amherst, Anna Buxton took her daughter East for the commencement ceremonies. Afterward, they stayed at the Boston YWCA and saw the sights, continuing on to Washington, D.C., where they stayed at the venerable Willard Hotel while they explored the national capital.

Ruth also visited her Berwyn, Illinois, cousins, one of whom (Hortense Kittleman) attended Girton, a girls' school. She said, "I thought I would like that too, but when I told my father I didn't want to go to Simpson, he was shocked. I finally realized that I had to consult my parents, and they won."

The child of two Simpson graduates with a father and grandfather on the college board and faculty members as family friends, Ruth Buxton naturally craved a change in the decision about her higher education, but she was a dutiful daughter.

Resigned to staying in Indianola, Ruth was glad to see her Aunt Pet, who was visiting from Berwyn, Illinois. The beautiful Pierce Arrow that Mrs. Little drove had been nursed along the rough roads with great care. When Aunt Pet came to a bridge, she would stop the car, send for a garage attendant and watch him drive the Pierce Arrow across the span

*Ruth was a loving big sister to William Buxton III
and Martha in 1913.*

before she would take the wheel again. Somehow she always was lucky
enough to find someone to do her bidding, probably because it was a
treat to take the wheel of such a car—even for a few moments.

In 1912 Ruth was vice-president of the junior class at Indianola
High School, and she played basketball, but, she said, "I wasn't that
good at it." She remembered the 1912 dedication of the Harry L.
Hopper Gymnasium on the Simpson campus chiefly because of the
hypnotic swaying of the feathers on Mrs. Hopper's hat.

In her high school senior year, Ruth Buxton's report card noted
that she was tardy four times in six weeks and absent seven and a half
days. Her marks were 97 in English, 95 in Virgil, 98 in German, and 99
in spelling.

Enrolled as a Simpson student, Ruth lived at home and walked ten
blocks to the campus every morning "no matter what the weather."
She was deprived of the kimono parties, midnight spreads, and pillow
fights in the dormitory, Mary Berry Hall, but she was pledged to her
mother's sorority, Pi Beta Phi, and the college newspaper reported,
"The Pi Phi's had a swell doings at the Buxtons last night."

Ruth's college wardrobe was acquired on shopping trips to Des
Moines by train and created by a dressmaker who lived a block from the

East Salem Street house. Mrs. Sayre said, "There were no stores in Indianola where you bought clothes."

The eventful fall of 1913 included the successful campaign of William Buxton, Jr., for the state legislature. He would be a member of the Iowa House of Representatives throughout Ruth's college years.

Simpson College attracted students from afar, but when it came to dating, Ruth Buxton chose the comfortable relationship with her old friend, Howard Smith.

Raymond Sayre's high school sweetheart was younger than he was, and the relationship between a college man and a high school girl became difficult to maintain. At this point, Howard Smith found it impossible to keep a date he had made with Ruth Buxton and asked Raymond Sayre to take his place.

Ruth immediately realized that she preferred Raymond Sayre to Howard Smith. Raymond—with a big Simpson "S" on his sweater, eloquence forged in college debate, and a warm manner—impressed her greatly, and she said, "I thought he was so much nicer, and I kept on going out with him. We went to sorority and fraternity parties (he was a Kappa Theta Psi), literary society programs, weekly services, social affairs of the Y, and to chapel, which was required. Evening chapel services were a sure date."

Chapel speakers emphasized the responsibility of individuals to use their abilities for the good of others, and Ruth was in the process of discovering what her abilities might be. She had done well in high school German, and her liking for Hildegarde Jend, the Simpson German professor, steered her to a major in that language. Miss Jend was a graduate of Wallace College in Berea, Ohio, with a master's degree from the University of Michigan.

Ruth was a member of the Zetalethean Literary Society, Simpson's oldest, founded in 1867, when the first question up for debate was "Resolved: That Women Should Be Given Equal Rights With Men." The winning view is not a matter of record, but in December 1875 a trial was held in Warren County to determine the eligibility of a woman, Elizabeth S. Cooke, to serve as county superintendent of schools. Eventually, Ms. Cooke's rights were vindicated, but not without the dissenting comment of W. H. Schooley: "The duties of county superintendent compel her to be traveling over the county at least 200 days in a year. The meagerness of the pay compels her to travel alone and unprotected." Schooley thought this should not be.

In later years this attempt to protect a "frail woman" against her own wishes might amuse Ruth Buxton Sayre, who traveled much farther alone and unprotected and with less recompense, but in her first college

*Ruth's sorority and her mother's, Pi Beta Phi,
initiated new members at the Buxton home.
Ruth is third from the left in the front row.*

*Raymond Sayre, the
Simpson College football
letterman, won the heart
of the banker's daughter.*

years the issue of women's rights was not her paramount concern. That would come later in the Simpson experience and beyond.

Raymond Sayre belonged to the Kallonian Literary Society, which was less venerable (founded in 1900) and somewhat less earnest in tone. The Kallonians compiled lists of the 120 great men of all time. The categories included bluffers, naming P. T. Barnum, Ananias, and Nero. Raymond also was a member of the debate team, and Mrs. Sayre said, "I took public speaking and did readings, but I didn't appreciate it much. I just wanted to show Raymond that I could do it as well as he could. He and some of the others were really good, but I found that I could hold my own with any man."

Ruth Buxton was secretary of her freshman class, which had a yell that compensated with spirit for its lack of substance: "Rackety Yackety Ackety Yack: Hullabaloo, Hullabaloo! How-Do-You-Do! Freshmen, Freshmen, Freshmen!"

A member of the college council, Ruth posed for a yearbook photo wearing a dark skirt, a high-collared white blouse, and a tentative smile, and she was pictured with the glee club looking clear-eyed and well-scrubbed.

During these years Ruth Buxton was exposed to uplifting words, both written and spoken, at Simpson College. An example is this "prayer" in the 1914 *Zenith*, the college yearbook: "To thee, O Spirit of Simpson, do we make our prayer: That we may be worthy of those in whose footsteps we are treading; that we may be able to count as our treasures deeds of kindness and words of cheer; that in times of darkness and adversity, we shall not fall by the wayside, but shall remain true to those ideals which shine before us as guiding stars; that we may be able to help a brother if, perchance, he be weaker than ourselves; that we may never know the bitterness of dishonorable defeat." To Ruth, such an exhortation sounded "just like home."

Words she would be less likely to hear at home came from Professor Aubrey W. Goodenough of the English department, regarded by many of the townspeople as a "radical." Goodenough, educated at Oberlin, Yale, and the University of Wisconsin, was, by the standards of the time and place, a Socialist. He espoused the writings of Carl Sandburg and prodded his students to question the status quo. Goodenough's influence stayed with Ruth Buxton Sayre throughout her life, tempering her conservative, Republican heritage.

Ruth worked hard for good grades to qualify as an honor student in English and German and to be eligible for Epsilon Sigma, the Honor Society. She was living the statement of the college president, Dr. Francis Strickland, "In college days the world grows bigger, horizons expand, convictions deepen."

The Buxton family's Franklin with Ruth at the wheel meant happy times for college friends.

The Simpson College YWCA was important to Ruth, seen here (seventh from the left) with other members at a summer gathering at Lake Geneva College.

If she had any religious doubts, Dr. William Hamilton with the strong voice and long, white beard of a Bible patriarch exorcised them in his Christian history classes. Mrs. Sayre said, "Nobody expressed doubts in his presence."

Ruth's grandfather, Claudius B. McLaughlin, died the day after Christmas in 1915. He had done all the housework while Grandma Jennie sat in a wicker chair with her ear horn, and no one had expected that he would be the first to go. Aunt Ida Metcalf, Anna Buxton's sister, took Grandma Jennie into her home, and Jane Anna Reynolds McLaughlin survived her husband less than a year, dying late in 1916.

In the final semester of Ruth's senior year at Simpson, the whole world was engulfed in doubt. On February 3, 1917, the United States broke off diplomatic relations with Germany because of unrestricted submarine warfare. On April 2, President Wilson asked for war. Even so, life went on.

Ruth was a teacher's assistant, and when Raymond came to call, he sometimes had the choice of helping her with the papers to be corrected or waiting longer while she finished them alone.

This also was the year when their mutual regard suffered a temporary strain. In both 1914 and 1916 the Votes for Women amendment had been passed by the Iowa General Assembly, then sent to the voters for a defeat laid to the door of areas heavily populated by German antiprohibition citizens. Carrie Chapman Catt, a former Iowan, was president of the National Woman Suffrage Association, and the movement gathered momentum in her native state.

Mrs. Sayre said, "A woman came from Des Moines to talk about women's rights at Simpson, and I helped organize our Woman's Suffrage groups. We marched around the Indianola square with banners that read 'Votes for Women,' and Raymond and his friends stood on the sidelines and catcalled. They lived to regret it!"

Years later when Jean Lloyd-Jones, then president of the Iowa League of Women Voters, spoke at an organizational meeting in Indianola, she referred to "our ancestors, the suffragettes." The voice of Ruth Buxton Sayre was loud and clear from the audience, "*I* was a suffragette, and I don't think of myself as your ancestor."

In 1917 with the world at war and commencement approaching, Ruth Buxton considered her situation. She had, she said, "no ambition past college other than getting married, having a home and children. I was going to teach until that happened." At that time she had no way of knowing that within a year Iowa's governor would issue an edict that only the English language be used in the state, rendering her German studies useless for the purpose of teaching.

"No one else I knew was going to marry a farmer," she said, "but I had heard so much about farming from my father, who owned farmland on all sides of Indianola, that I thought farming was all right."

If Ruth Buxton had needed reassurance, she might have read the words of the Reverend W. C. Martin in his 1908 *History of Warren County:* "There is something in the cultivation of the soil that stimulates thought and widens one's vision and prepares him for contemplating the highest and best interests of humanity."

She was graduated from Simpson College June 4, 1917, at 2:30 p.m. The motto of the class of 1917 was "Excelsior!" and its colors were old rose and green. Dr. James W. Campbell gave the invocation, and Cloyd Conner delivered an oration entitled "The Negro Problem," followed by Elva May's presentation of her prize-winning piece of oratory, "The Rights of the Child." A third speaker was Bert O. Lyle, who offered "Gambrinus's Farewell." Ruth, who had long since abandoned the piano, may have felt the resurgence of an old rancor when Ilo Moore played the soulful "Meditation" from Thais, triggering memories of Ilo Browne, the practicing paragon who had so greatly impressed her mother. The Buxton Oratorical Prize was awarded, as was the Buxton Scholarship, and at last the precious scroll was in Ruth Buxton's hand. She was educated—well-schooled in the German language—and her country was at war with Germany.

Raymond had planned to take a training course at Estes Park in Colorado for war service with the YMCA, but when the Y secretary at Iowa State College in Ames went to war, Raymond was asked to take his place instead of going west. Now he and Ruth were about 50 miles apart, and she knew it would get worse because he had applied for Officers' Training School.

Public school teachers came and went rapidly in this unsettled period, opening a teaching position for Ruth at Indianola High School. She said, "As a new recruit, I was given the classes no one else wanted, including the Normal Training class for girls preparing to be rural teachers. I had never been in a rural school, and somehow I hadn't realized how poorly taught they were until I encountered these girls who couldn't speak the English language properly. One of them couldn't get *anything* right, and I couldn't imagine how she should hope to teach pupils in a country school."

Ruth Buxton did what she could for the Normal Training students, and she considered it to be very little, but she would remember their plight in years to come and put up a vigorous fight for the improvement of rural education.

Her students in that first year of teaching were slow in English and history, which was discourgaing. Correcting papers in the Salem Street house at night, she would glance at her sister Martha and her brother Bill as they studied in the soft lamplight and envy *their* teachers.

Anna Buxton said soothingly, "Now Ruth, those girls of yours haven't had the same advantages."

"I know," Ruth said with a sigh, but she didn't know the half of it yet.

Raymond was coming, and she hurried to finish the papers and go upstairs to get dressed. The best part of her teaching job was the salary, $75 a month, which was the first money she ever had been allowed to spend as she pleased. Part of a month's check had purchased a straw hat with a crown of flowers and a blue georgette dress.

When Raymond arrived he was bursting with untold news, and Ruth thought it best to listen before asking how he liked her new dress. As it happened, the dress was forgotten when he told her that orders had come through and he was to report to the Officers' Training camp of the Coast Artillery at Fort Monroe, Virginia.

Their parting was tender and much too soon. Ruth was dismayed by his fervent hope that he would be sent overseas when he received his commission, but this was a righteous war, and Raymond had righteous instincts. She could not expect him to feel otherwise.

Letters from Indianola and Fort Monroe passed each other in the mails, carrying messages of love and the first actual mention of eventual marriage. Somehow the school year passed, and it was summer. The wedding planned for "after the war" seemed very far away.

In September Raymond wrote that he was now a second lieutenant, and he was to be sent to the Coast Defenses at Puget Sound rather than to France. His disappointment was evident, but Ruth rejoiced privately, and she noticed that his spirits rose as it occurred to him that they might marry sooner—if he could find a place where they could live near the army post. He investigated the possibilities thoroughly, was assured of a room in a captain's quarters at Fort Worden on Puget Sound, and wrote to Ruth saying that he would be in Indianola for a week on his way to Washington State. Could they be married during that week?

Ruth's answer was "Yes!" and she and her mother threw themselves into the hectic business of preparing for a wedding in a week's time. The date was to be October 4, and the ceremony would have to be in the evening, because the father of the bride had promised to take tickets at the county fair in the afternoon. As one of the fair's backers, he could not renege on his duty.

Anna Buxton found a dressmaker who could create a wedding gown on short notice and managed to collect enough sugar—so scarce in

Lieutenant Raymond Sayre was in army uniform for his marriage to Ruth Buxton on October 4, 1918. Although Ruth's wedding costume was created in a hurry, no elegant detail was slighted.

wartime—to have a wedding cake made. The Salem Street house was cleaned and polished with special attention to the parlor, where the vows would be said beneath the vaulting turret.

Ruth found a substitute to teach her high school classes, Mrs. Mabel Billingsley, and she asked her sister Martha to serve as maid of honor. The Scroggs twins, Alice and Agnes, were recruited to scatter rose petals, and Raymond's little sister, Mary Elizabeth, who was eighteen years younger than he, was to be the ring bearer.

By some miracle, all was in readiness when the bridegroom arrived from Virginia. The ceremony was set for 8:30 p.m., and promptly at that moment the strains of Mendelssohn were heard. As Raymond entered the parlor in the uniform of a United States Army lieutenant, his puttees squeaked.

Ruth smiled at the sound as she took the arm of her father. She wore a street-length gown of white embroidered crepe georgette over white silk designed with a Pilgrim neckline. A white silk cap held her tulle veil, and she carried white roses and valley lilies.

The Scroggs twins scattered rose petals from pink satin baskets along the bride's path to a parlor decorated with autumn leaves, white clematis, and lighted candles. Martha, dressed in white organdy over pink satin, held a sheaf of pink Killarney roses. She smiled tremulously at her sister while Dr. F. W. Willis, the Methodist pastor, gave the soldier bridegroom a look of encouragement.

One special face was missing from the assembly of loved ones. Grandpa Buxton had died March 5, 1918, while vacationing in Long Beach, and Ruth's father still was struggling with the settling of his estate, a matter complicated by California community property probate law.

At the proper moment, Ruth said in a clear voice, "I do," and seven-year-old Mary Elizabeth Sayre solemnly proffered the ring that would make her a very young sister-in-law.

Later, when the wedding cake had been cut and the Pi Phi's were serving the guests, the bride thought of the biblical Ruth whose name she shared and the familiar words that now took on new meaning, "Whither thou goest, I will go."

4

Whither Thou Goest

LIEUTENANT and Mrs. Raymond Sayre made their own Lewis and Clark expedition to the Northwest, followed by dire warnings from friends and relatives that a flu epidemic was sure to strike the Puget Sound military installation. This was, in fact, the case, and the Sayres hastened to be inoculated against the Spanish influenza.

Their one-room home in a captain's quarters at Fort Worden did not require much housekeeping, and they took their meals in the officers' mess. After mastering military etiquette and putting it to use in a formal call on the Fort Worden commander and his wife, Ruth volunteered to teach a Sunday School class of officers' children and spent hours making flu masks.

The newlyweds found time to stroll in the "thousands of lovers' lanes," to admire the scenery, and occasionally to visit Port Townsend, which Ruth described in a letter home as "the deadest little place I ever saw. It has one dry goods store and no dry goods."

She became acquainted with other young officers' wives, including "one who looks like a vamp and is a terrible gossip" and another "who 'my dears' you to death."

The Fort Worden barracks were filled with young soldiers stricken by the flu, and death was a constant occurrence at the post. The pall of mourning for so many young men tainted the pleasure the Sayres otherwise would have taken in their new surroundings on the salt water inland sea that is Puget Sound: greening rains, mild temperatures, flowers, evergreen forests, and the snowy Cascades. On a clear day they could see Mt. Rainier.

On November 11, 1918, when the rest of the world was rejoicing, Fort Worden was too shattered by death and illness to celebrate the signing of the Armistice beyond the breathing of a quiet "Thank God!"

Ruth and Raymond escaped the contagion and were home for Christmas in Indianola, a joyous celebration with both families.

Raymond always had planned to go back to the land his grandfather, Enoch Sayre, had homesteaded in 1856 near New Virginia, but his friends in YMCA work now tried to persuade him to make a career in the Y. Another prospect was the offer of a bank job from Ruth's father, who was establishing his own bank, Peoples Trust and Savings, in 1919.

Ruth Sayre did not try to tip the scales one way or the other, believing that her husband should follow his strongest inclination. The move would be postponed for a time, at least, because Raymond had promised to return to Ames, where the YMCA still was without a secretary, until someone else could be found to fill that position.

The months that followed would be the last in which Ruth would enjoy electricity and running water for more than a decade, but she took these amenities for granted as she prepared for the move to the farm.

She removed the white and gold paint from Grandma McLaughlin's walnut chairs and caned them. They were the first of her family antiques, to be joined later by Grandpa Buxton's gentleman's chair. She said, "I can still see him sitting in it in front of the fireplace reading. Then he would wind the clock and go to bed."

There had been no time to work on the obligatory embroidered pillow cases and dresser runners before the wedding, and Ruth did this while Raymond was working in Ames. She also preserved countless quarts of peaches, pears, and tomatoes to take to the farm.

She said, "I had been told that I wouldn't get into town very often, but I didn't really take this in, not even when I saw the kitchen cabinet with a bin that would hold a whole sack of flour."

The village of New Virginia, laid out in 1856 and formally located in 1859, consisted of a post office, two churches, a Masonic Lodge, a hotel, and a blacksmith shop. Raymond's grandfather had been a charter member of the Methodist church, where the text for the first sermon was "Stand fast in the faith. Quit ye yourselves like men."

That challenge still held when Ruth and Raymond Sayre moved to the family farm in November 1919. The house with a wide porch of ornamentally carved wood faced east with two gables to the south. This was the second house on the property, built by Raymond's parents with four rooms originally, then the addition of a kitchen and two other

*The New Virginia farmhouse where the newly-
weds moved in 1919 had been Raymond Sayre's
boyhood home.*

rooms. Raymond's Aunt Minnie Anderson lived in the original house,
which had two porches and steep gables.

The Sayres established their life together in a home lighted by coal
oil lamps and heated by wood-burning stoves. Mrs. Sayre said, "The
running water was the kind you run after, and the plumbing was of the
outdoor variety. The house was big and cold until you started the
range."

Upstairs were three bedrooms and a storeroom, and in that first
winter, they discovered it was too cold to sleep anywhere but the
southeast room, where the stovepipe passed through. As the mercury
continued to plummet, they slept in the living room, opening its door
to the dining room, which had a stove.

Faced with more primitive conditions than she was accustomed to,

Ruth Sayre was determined to make it impossible for anyone to say (or even think) that Raymond had made a mistake in marrying a "town girl." Raymond taught her how to fire a wood stove, but it was Aunt Minnie Anderson who came to her rescue when she was baffled by the myriad duties of a farm homemaker.

"In the old days," she said, "we had to butcher after Christmas, render lard, and smoke or can meat. Aunt Minnie taught me how to cut up meat and fry down sausages. And I had to learn to make soap, because I didn't want to waste all that grease."

When her Rhode Island Reds hatched a clutch of eggs as early as any chickens in the neighborhood, Ruth Sayre decided that she was getting the hang of being a farm wife. Raymond's instructions on how to set the hens, how to distinguish one wood from another for the heater, and how to keep it going had been right on the mark, and she was an apt pupil.

Ruth was young, strong, and equal to the hard labor of farm life, but as she churned butter, rendered lard, cleaned lamp chimneys, carried water, washed with her mother's old scrubbing board and copper boiler, helped put up ice from a pond north of the house ("the coldest job there was!"), and prepared breakfast in a kitchen "cold as Greenland's icy mountain!" Ruth Sayre remembered Professor Goodenough's contention that change was possible.

"I didn't fuss at Raymond and think I had a hard life on the farm," she said. "That was the way other country people were living. But I thought I could make it better."

Her first brush with the resigned inertia of country people came about in a conversation with Aunt Minnie Anderson. Mrs. Sayre said, "I had a new, shiny Copper Clad range; a new oak kitchen cabinet, bright curtains, and shiny linoleum, and I thought it was like a magazine picture.

"Then winter came with armloads of wood scattering dust and chips; milk pails and separators brought in so they wouldn't freeze; men's winter coats, sweaters and overshoes; and later baby pigs and lambs near the stove. In the spring, my baby chicks were almost drowned in the rain, and they came into the kitchen. My dream kitchen. My magazine picture vanished, and I complained."

Aunt Minnie smiled sympathetically, then sighed deeply and said, "Ruth, you can't have it any other way on the farm."

It occurred to Ruth Sayre that the "can't have it" philosophy applied not only to her kitchen, but to education, churches, and living standards for farm people.

"They didn't think about what they could do to change things," she said. "Their fathers had done things that way and their grandfathers before that, and there was no other way."

Ruth Sayre rejected the "can't have it" outlook, but it would be some time before she could engage in active battle against it. Soon there would be a huge garden to plant, then canning to stock the cave near the house for the next winter. There would be trips to town over mud roads by wagon for supplies and chickens to tend.

Raymond was Sunday School superintendent at the Methodist church, where Ruth was active in women's work, and he rode to the church on horseback when the weather prevented the use of a wagon. Mrs. Sayre said, "He thought he had to be there, and he was, no matter what!"

The Sayres raised corn, cattle, and hogs on the New Virginia farm, and Raymond always enjoyed having some sheep. Mrs. Sayre said, "The land at New Virginia was not so good, and we had to make our living on livestock, though we did raise some grain."

When Ruth Sayre took her first turn at feeding threshers, she tried to give the occasion at least a touch of the elegance of an East Salem Street dinner with a table arrangement of nasturtiums. When one of the farmers picked up the flowers and passed them as a joke, she bit her tongue and resolved to reserve touches of beauty for those who could appreciate them.

She never, however, lost sight of the necessity for beauty in daily living, which Raymond appreciated. She was fortunate in having married a man like the ideal love described by Marian the librarian in Meredith Willson's *The Music Man,* one who wouldn't "be ashamed of a few nice things."

They were close in every way, and as Ruth Sayre said many years later, "A husband and wife living on a farm naturally have the same interests—all that goes on at the farm is of mutual concern. Our farm is our home and our business. We talk things over and reach our decisions together."

The Depression hit farmers nearly a decade before the rest of the nation felt its effects. The young Sayres had borrowed money at seven percent interest to buy into partnership with Raymond's father, and they soon realized that their livestock and grain were bringing prices less than half the amount invested in them. How would they ever pay their debt?

They saved in every possible way, amusing themselves by reading and listening in on the party line and going without everything but the

Looking like anything but a hardworking farmwife,
Ruth Sayre posed with her firstborn child on
Helen's first birthday in January 1921.

barest essentials. Even so, Mrs. Sayre said, "There was never enough money. Even if we denied ourselves everything, there were Saturday nights when we couldn't pay the hired man."

They did what they could with what they had. Ruth learned canning and cold-packing techniques from Extension leaders, beginning her lifelong love affair with these teachers of a better way to use available resources.

The Sayres were expecting their first child, and their daughter Helen arrived January 29, 1920, delivered by Dr. George Alden in his hospital rooms above the beer parlor on the Indianola square. Recalling the birth, Mrs. Sayre said, "I guess it was hard, but not that bad."

Raymond kept house alone for three weeks while Ruth was in the hospital, cooking for the man hired to help pick corn (hand picking brought the crop in much later in those days), making ten plate-sized pancakes for breakfast every morning.

Bringing a new baby to her New Virginia home, which was "a typical farmhouse" of the period, Ruth Sayre fought the winter cold by carrying wood and hauling water to wash diapers "with Raymond's help, of course," she said.

Sometimes she would look at the bathtub Raymond's parents had installed in the addition and sigh. The tub had a drain, but it had to be filled by dipping water from the reservoir, a seemingly endless task.

One frigid night Raymond brought the milk separator into the kitchen with its contents frozen solid. Who could know that the spigot was open? In the morning, water was everywhere, and the neighbors had to be called to lift the stove while Ruth wiped up the mess.

When they took the team and wagon to town for supplies, the fire would go out in their absence, and Mrs. Sayre said, "I always hated going home to a cold house!"

But spring with its baby chicks and gardening was on its way, and the chill of the house soon was just a memory. When the hired man came down with the measles, Ruth disked the south field with a gentle team and found it more pleasant than working in a hot, steamy kitchen. She never learned to milk a cow, however, and she said, "There was no good reason for letting myself in for that chore."

In late August 1920 ratification of the right to vote for women was completed, and Ruth Sayre was intensely interested in the fact that the first woman to vote in Iowa and possibly the first in the nation was Mrs. Jens G. Thuesen, who cast her ballot in a rural school reorganization election near Cedar Falls. Ruth soon had her own chance to exercise this basic right, riding five miles over mud roads in a wagon to vote for school consolidation in New Virginia.

Raymond experimented with beekeeping, and Mrs. Sayre said, "I tried to help, but I did everything wrong."

The season turned, and it was time to start picking corn by hand and to prepare for the rigors of another winter. That fall, Ruth Sayre conceived again.

Alice was born in the spring of 1921, delivered by Dr. George Jardine at home. Mrs. Sayre said, "Alice came when Raymond's father was very sick. We went to see him every Sunday, and the nurse who cared for him was with me when Alice arrived. The phone didn't work that morning, and Raymond had to ride to the neighbors to call the doctor, who barely made it because of bad roads. I heard Raymond calling his aunt. He said, 'Aunt Minnie, it's another little girl.' He was expecting a boy."

Raymond's father, Will Sayre, died immediately after Alice's birth, and Ruth was unable to attend the funeral services.

The expected son had turned out to be a daughter, and it occurred to Ruth Sayre that very few expectations were being met that year. When Raymond sold hogs, she would ask anxiously, "How much did you get?'' His answer became standard, ''Not as much as I expected to—but I didn't expect to.''

Their individual effort with its hard work and thrift was getting them nowhere. Was there some way to band together with other farmers to improve their lot? Many of Ruth Sayre's elders thought not, accepting the blows of circumstance with stoicism, but she remembered Professor Aubrey Goodenough with hair receding on one side and rising in a springy tuft on the other. It had been hard to see the set of his mouth beneath a luxuriant mustache, but his eyes had the far-reaching gaze of a visionary. ''You can change things!'' he had said, and she had believed him then. She believed him now. There must be a way.

5

Changing Things

THE way presented itself in the form of a letter from the Warren County Farm Bureau office inviting Ruth Sayre to an organizational meeting for women in March 1922.

The Sayres now had their own Model T Ford with isinglass windows and flapping curtains to make the twenty-five mile trip to Indianola, but it had no heater, and a late winter journey with a two-year-old and an infant in arms was a formidable undertaking.

That March day marked the first time Anna Buxton took care of her grandchildren in her daughter's long span of volunteer service. Ruth Sayre's younger son, John, says, "She couldn't have done all the things she did without the love and support of her own mother." The children were with Anna Buxton so much that they called her "Mamma," and Ruth Sayre was "Mother."

The American Farm Bureau Federation, one of four large organizations representing the nation's farm interests, had a membership of large and small farm owners, and it projected a moderate, sensible view of farm problems and their possible solutions that appealed to Ruth Sayre. In later years she was fond of referring to the Farm Bureau as the most important piece of "furniture" in the Sayre household.

When she came home from the Indianola meeting, Raymond said, "Well, Ruth, how did you get along?" In time, this welcome-home question would be appropriated by their son John, who said, "Well, how did you get along, Mother?" every time his maternal parent returned from a trip or a meeting.

Ruth's answer that first day was, "I'm the new Farm Bureau chairman for Virginia Township!"

Raymond asked what the job involved, and she explained that she must organize Virginia Township to take advantage of the Iowa State College Extension courses available to rural women. The approach was to find five local leaders to attend Extension lesson meetings and pass the information along at neighborhood meetings. She also was to find a "cooperator" in each of the township's nine school districts.

Ruth intended to begin recruiting immediately, and the next morning she said somewhat apologetically, "Daddy, would you mind eating a cold dinner if I don't get home in time to cook?"

Raymond told her that would be fine, and years later she said, "He didn't know how many cold dinners he would be eating through the years, nor did I."

Bundling the little girls into the Ford, Ruth drove through the hills of the township with great expectations. She was sold on the idea of the new Home Project with the Extension Service and was confident that other farm women would share her enthusiasm. The day was young; her daughters were dry, rested, and recently fed, and she hoped to accomplish her mission so quickly that Raymond would have a decent dinner after all.

Ruth turned into the lane of the first prospect's farm home and parked the Ford in the rutted yard. With Alice in one arm and Helen clutching her hand, she was grateful for the barking dog that obviated the necessity of knocking on the door.

The farm wife invited her in, and they sat near a quilting frame while Ruth Sayre explained the opportunity of working with Extension and said, "We'd like you to be one of the local leaders."

The woman threw up her hands. "Oh, I couldn't!" she said, sliding a glance at the quilting frame, which held a partially finished quilt in the double wedding ring pattern, "There's that—and I have to paint the kitchen and pantry, and my cousin Edna is coming for two weeks, and—"

Ruth Sayre said, "She went on with a long list of all the things she had to do, and it made me tired just to hear about it. I told her I would get someone else, put the children in the car, and drove on."

The ruts in the road were treacherous, gravel hit the car body with great force and Alice needed a diaper change, which was accomplished when they reached the next farm. Admitted to the house and offered a cup of tea, Ruth told her story again, thinking it sounded irresistible. "And we'd like you to be one of the local leaders."

Fingers fluttering at her throat, the farm wife said, "I couldn't possibly do that. I—I'm not very well, you see." A description of symptoms followed, and the recital was more than a little distasteful to a Buxton taught not to give in to physical infirmity or even the mention of it.

Helen's small hand was reaching for a corner of the tablecloth to pull herself up from the floor, but Ruth caught her in time to avert the destruction of the teacups. Fastening coats and bonnets, she said, "Thank you for the tea. We'd better go and give you a chance to lie down. I do hope you feel better soon."

Less optimistic by now, Ruth approached still another farmhouse and explained how Extension could teach new ways of doing things if women in the township would cooperate. The woman listened with shining eyes, and Ruth dared to hope until she said, "I would love to be a leader, but I can't. John wouldn't want me to do anything like that."

"Why not?" Ruth asked, thinking of Raymond obligingly consenting to the cold dinner he was increasingly likely to get.

"Oh, he thinks I have plenty to keep me busy in our own home. He doesn't want me to do *anything* on the outside."

Ruth sighed inwardly but said nothing, feeling thankful that Raymond had a keen sense of man's responsibility to man and wanted to be part of making things better for others.

As the day wore on, she heard variations on the themes of refusal, and at dusk, she headed for home without committing even one woman to being a local leader. The girls were wailing dismally, and Ruth Sayre's thoughts were bleak, but as she reviewed the day, it occurred to her that she had liked many of the women she had visited. They were down-to-earth, genuine, hard-working, and dependable, but they were also conservative, unwilling to fling themselves into a new venture without studied consideration. What they needed was to hear the story again and again until it was no longer a new thing.

When she got home, Raymond took the weeping Alice from her arms and said, "Well, Ruth, how did you get along?"

She shook her head. "I didn't accomplish what I set out to do, but I realized that I'll have to begin where I am with what I have."

Roger Fleming, longtime secretary-treasurer of the American Farm Bureau Federation, says, "I have marveled at Mrs. Sayre's sensitivity for people. It came through in private conversation and public speeches. She was 'people oriented' long before it became fashionable."

That sensitivity prevented her from arguing with the refusals of farm wives and shutting the door to future approaches. Slowly, one by one, Ruth Sayre found her leaders.

The women of Virginia Township began studying home nursing with the county Red Cross nurse, learning the value of hot lunches in schools, and profiting from cheese-making demonstrations. They took particular interest in making dress forms, producing twenty-five of them in that township alone.

Extension outreach drove the first wedge in the belief of rural women that things must always be as they have always been. It threatened the "can't have it" complex, much to Ruth Sayre's delight. Extension was the educational arm of the Farm Bureau, which provided its funding base, teaching farm women that their families could live better in better farm homes than their parents, grandparents, and more remote ancestors had been able to do.

Women who had had no opportunity for high school or college education were learning eagerly, becoming intelligent consumers as well as independent producers. Ruth Sayre saw the practical courses as a foundation for leadership training. Once the women were organized, there should be no limit to what they could do. Beginning where she was with what she had, Ruth Sayre was moving ahead and getting more.

Years later she said, "Virginia Township, Irish Grove school district, was where my work began, and it always remained the focal point for me. Problems were interpreted on the basis of this local human experience. What I learned from the women in Virginia Township was my basic training in human relations."

Mrs. Sayre's Farm Bureau responsibilities took time, but she still managed her home well and even helped in the fields when Raymond was hard pressed. She would drive the Ford to the field and use it as a playpen for the two little girls while she helped the preacher's son who stayed with them in the summer make hay. Her job was to lead the horse. She said, "Once a year I would help plow after I put the children to sleep."

In August 1924 the son Raymond had waited for was born to the Sayres, delivered by Dr. George Jardine in the New Virginia farmhouse. Mrs. Sayre said, "I didn't have enough milk to nurse Bill, so I prepared formula and kept it in the cave. Bill was born at threshing time, and the neighbors took over for me when it was my turn to feed the crew."

The Sayres discussed the purchase of a tractor to improve the efficiency of field work, but, Mrs. Sayre said, "My father wasn't sure it was the right thing to do. He was a very conservative fellow."

In 1925 Ruth Sayre stepped up on the Farm Bureau ladder, becoming county chairman of the Women's Committee, and this meant recruiting leaders in a larger territory. She traveled with Neale S. Knowles, state Home Economics Extension leader, to seventeen townships for organization meetings, learning much from the businesslike approach of the woman responsible for the successful Iowa

Ruth Sayre's mother, Anna Buxton, kept Alice, Helen, and the baby Bill happy while their mother was busy with Farm Bureau duties in 1924.

plan of organizing Home Project programs in rural areas. Anna Buxton cared for the infant Bill while his mother was away.

Later Ruth Sayre returned to all the townships for meetings, driving the country roads in all kinds of weather. Once when she took Bill along, the car stalled on the way home. She said, "Nobody stopped to help, and I started to walk home carrying the baby. Finally, a woman picked us up. The road between Indianola and New Virginia was bad with a sharp curve at the bottom of the hill, but they finally paved it halfway."

For seven years, Ruth Sayre served as county Home Project chairman, spending at least fifty days a year on the details of the office which was combined with the vice-presidency of the county Farm Bureau. She said, "We had no Home Demonstration agent, so I did that work with the help of the county agent."

In her kitchen hung a Warren County map with every organized township starred. The homes, churches, and schools where she attended meetings also were marked, and the Sayre children learned their earliest lessons in geography from "Mother's map." By this time Helen was old enough to involve Alice in "going to meeting" games, which seemed much more real to them than playing house.

The women of Warren County moved from making dress forms and learning to handle pressure cookers to studies on the latest developments in nutrition, home furnishings, and home management.

The sturdy family home at Ackworth was only ten years old when the Sayres moved in. Sheltering trees and a rolling vista to the South River made it a pleasant dwelling.

By 1928 the county had seventy-five active leaders who had held 468 meetings to pass information along to nearly 4,000 women.

In addition to Home Project work, the county program included sponsoring baby clinics in cooperation with the University of Iowa, promoting smallpox vaccination, and supporting the 4-H Club. The Farm Bureau Women's Committee helped organize new 4-H clubs and found leaders for them in many of the Warren County townships.

Ruth Sayre was deeply committed to the 4-H program, not only because she knew her children would be involved in it as soon as they were old enough but because its aims and ideals were in line with her own. A photograph of the late 1920s shows a slender Ruth Sayre participating in a 4-H ceremony at the Iowa State Fair.

Attending countless Achievement Days and County Annual Meetings where oyster stew and creamed chicken on biscuits were served would in time change that willowy form to the more substantial figure associated with farm cooking and its liberal use of butter, cream, and eggs.

On August 26, 1929, Ruth Sayre received the Community Service Award of the *Des Moines Register,* an Iowa newspaper with a statewide circulation. The citation read, "Ruth Buxton Sayre is entitled to recognition for distinguished service in Warren County, Iowa, for her contribution in making her home and her community a better place in which to live. This award is sponsored by the *Register* and *Tribune,* Iowa State Fair, and cooperating farm organizations."

One of the first recognitions of Ruth Sayre's community housekeeping, this award made her more determined than ever to wake up farm women and push them beyond the horizons of husband, home, and children.

Also in 1929 the Sayres made the decision to move to a farm belonging to Ruth's father near Ackworth in East Lincoln Township. Although he never spoke of it, Ruth knew that Raymond had regrets about leaving the farm of his pioneer grandfather. Even so, he believed they had made a practical choice. Ruth was overjoyed, because the new farm was only five miles from Indianola. The nine-room house, which faced north, was large, well-built, and less than ten years old. Sunrise streamed into the kitchen windows, and the back of the house over-looked an expanse of fields stretching to the South River.

She said, "We paid rent to my father, and I don't remember a time when it wasn't difficult. We started very far down."

Ackworth, with a population of 100, was laid out in 1874. In 1929 it included a Friends church, a post office where the Sayres picked up their mail, a school, a grocery, and a blacksmith shop. The big stone wheels from Bundy's old mill could still be seen, and on the Sayres' new farm just west of the village were the foundation stones of the log cabin which was the birthplace of the first white child born in Warren County, a son of the Paris A. Hendersons.

Ruth was interested to learn that Ackworth Institute, a Quaker school founded in 1869, had started its library with donations from England. No longer in existence, the school had aimed "to develop in pupils a high moral purpose, true self-reliance, and an energy and determination that will not shrink from the difficult but achieve success as the measure of merit."

Wishing that Ackworth Institute had survived, Ruth Sayre was sorry that the move had uprooted her own children from the consolidation at New Virginia and returned them to a one-room schoolhouse. The Ackworth school actually had an attached playroom, which made it a two-room schoolhouse technically, but it offered a one-room education.

The furniture scarcely had been moved into the new house when the family was plunged into grief by the death of Old Ring, the collie dog Raymond had given to Ruth on their first Christmas at New Virginia. Ten years old and bewildered by strange territory, Ring was struck and killed by a passing car. After appropriate funeral services, Ring's grieving family buried him in the orchard, and they never allowed another pet to claim as much of their hearts.

Soon after the move, the Sayres bought a tin-can sealer which Raymond operated, putting the cans into a boiler in the basement. This was the kind of progress encouraged by Extension, and Ruth and Raymond were optimistic about the constant improvement of their home and farming operation.

The year 1929 was not propitious for such development. Hogs were selling for three cents a pound, corn was bringing twelve cents a bushel, and farms were being lost when there was no money for taxes or mortgage payments. Mercifully, the Sayres did not realize that conditions would worsen before they got better. Things were bad enough as they were.

Ruth busied herself with the organization of the Ackworth PTA for the sake of her own children and others, and she began to identify the needs she would remember in her future efforts on the School Code Commission: higher qualifications for teachers, hot lunches, and a school bus system.

Ruth Sayre did remember one joyous occurrence in the year of the Crash. The Ackworth farmhouse was wired for electricity, and, she said, "I turned lights on all over the house that first night, and I felt richer than I ever did before or since. Why, I could see into corners!"

6

Moving Up

IN 1930, the year Grant Wood's painting of a dour Iowa farm couple—*American Gothic*—became a world sensation, Ruth Buxton Sayre began to present her own special image of an Iowa farm woman beyond her home county.

Roger Fleming has said, "She was eager to be an effective leader. This was her nature." Ruth Sayre's nature also called for an intense and loving concentration on home and family, and the marriage of these two drives resulted in a letter from *The Farmer's Wife* magazine in St. Paul, Minnesota, informing her that she had been nominated for the designation of Master Farm Homemaker.

The honor had been established in 1927 at the suggestion of Dan Wallace, editor of *The Farmer's Wife,* with the statement, "There can be no Master Farmers unless there are also Master Homemakers because farm success comes from the working out of a real partnership between the farmer and his wife. During the coming year, *The Farmer's Wife* proposes to conduct a national study of efficient rural homemaking. Five women are to be chosen from each state, nominated for this honor by friends and neighbors. They must be actual farm women carrying the responsibility of a farm home."

In 1927 Iowa ranked first in the number of nominations; the selection was to be made in 1928. The magazine pointed out, "This is not a contest or a race. These women are typical of thousands of others. Each has taken the particular circumstances with which she was faced and molded them to her purpose."

The search for Master Farm Homemakers was well publicized, and

*In the late 1920s, Bill, Helen, and Alice preferred
playing "going to a meeting like Mother" to other
childhood games.*

The Farmer's Wife noted, "This recognition of the real place of all farm
women brings them increased responsibility—responsibility for using
their powers of thought and action for the building of the very best
rural life."

Readers in Warren County were struck by the thought that Ruth
Buxton Sayre had all the qualities ascribed to a Master Farm Homemaker. Five signers were necessary for a nomination, and many times
that number could have been found.

Mrs. Sayre was stunned by the 56-page work sheet that soon arrived
at the Ackworth post office, but she went at it, answering questions
about the training of her children, her philosophy of life, and whether
her home was happy. Possessed of the natural reticence of the Buxtons,
she considered some of the questions too personal, but she answered
them as best she could. They ranged from "How high from the floor are
the seats of the privy?" to "What are you doing to give spiritual train-

ing in the home?" Other questions were concerned with what kind of neighbor she was and whether her family was "so trained that you can leave them at times when duty calls you elsewhere."

Questions about the home counted only 100 out of 1,000 points, and the heavy emphasis was on social development and community service. Ruth remembered a statement in *The Farmer's Wife* that she had agreed with wholly and adopted for her own: "Most farm women realize that community homemaking is quite as important as individual homemaking. True community spirit is just an overflow of love in the home—eager and anxious to share its blessings with others."

The work sheet was sent to the Extension Service at Iowa State College, and in due course, Ruth Buxton Sayre was summoned to Ames for the two-day program in which the honor would be conferred. Her fellow Master Farm Homemakers from Iowa were Mrs. Etha Koehler, Van Meter; Mrs. Alvern S. Wendell, Bronson; Mrs. Clarence H. Decatur, Grinnell; and Mrs. Albert S. Jacobson, Jewell. Raymond went with her to Ames and beamed with quiet pride as the rest of the world caught on to what he had known for a long time.

Six-year-old Bill Sayre was deeply impressed by his mother's new honor. The story about it in the Indianola newspaper and his teacher's remark that she had seen an account of it in an out-of-town paper were something to brag about, which he did with great enthusiasm.

The pattern of Ruth Buxton Sayre's life was not yet clear, but those who knew her had an intimation that she would rise to the top like cream in any organization that attracted her energies. Within a few years she would be president of the Master Homemakers Guild.

In 1930 she also climbed another rung on the Farm Bureau ladder, becoming district chairman of the Iowa State Farm Bureau Women's Committee. She represented District Eight, ten counties in south central Iowa. She said, "From the standpoint of soil resources, income, and leadership, it was considered to be one of the poorer sections of the state," but she was undaunted by the demography of her district. She would, as usual, begin where she was with what she had.

As a reward for her county Farm Bureau labors, Ruth Sayre was sent to the 1930 American Farm Bureau Federation annual convention in Boston. Since she had visited that eastern city with her mother at the time of Raymond Cooper's graduation, she felt less urgent about seeing the sights of the historic city than some of the other delegates. She devoted herself to representing the Warren County Farm Bureau and bringing the convention back alive to its members.

The ideal of farm people working together became a reality for Ruth Sayre in Boston. Ed O'Neal, president of the American Farm Bureau Federation, spoke with a disarming southern accent, but his words described the harsh truth about the condition of farmers and issued a tough appeal for action.

Mrs. Charles Sewell, who had been state chairman of the Indiana Farm Bureau women and was administrative director of the Associated Women of the American Farm Bureau Federation, was there too, and Mrs. Sayre said, "I was a little bit in awe of her. Everybody called her 'Mamma Sewell.' "

The formidable "Mamma Sewell" would, in later years, send Ruth Sayre a birthday poem that began, "There once was a baby named Ruthie / Who showed promise 'ere she cut her first toothie. . . . " Before that close friendship was forged, Mrs. Sayre was content to admire Mrs. Sewell's speaking ability from a distance.

The Boston meeting also was the occasion of Ruth Sayre's introduction to the Associated Country Women of the World. The international organization had been conceived by the Marchioness of Aberdeen and Temair and Mrs. Alfred Watt in Canada, organized in London in 1929, and launched with its first conference in Vienna in 1930.

Mrs. Edward Young of the New York delegation reported to the convention on the Vienna conference, telling how rural women from thirty-four organizations in twenty-eight countries had met to find ways to improve the lot of country women throughout the world.

The hardships of small farmers in Canada had reminded Lady Aberdeen of the difficult life of the crofters in her native Scotland, and she found a partner in her concern in Mrs. Alfred Watt, who had come to Canada from England during World War I. They met at Squire Hall, Stoney Creek, not far from Toronto to formulate a way to serve rural women.

Ruth Sayre was electrified by the idea of her own aims enlarged to a worldwide scope. The "can't have it" attitude now could be attacked around the globe. Miss Grace Frysinger, a senior home economist with the United States Department of Agriculture and a vice-president of the Associated Country Women of the World, was urging United States rural women's groups to join the international body and attend the second triennial meeting in Stockholm in 1933, but many of them would hold back for a few years. Like the women of Virginia Township, they needed to think about it for a while.

The Boston AFBF convention deepened Ruth Sayre's commitment to the farm cause. She said, "I knew I was part of something bigger than myself—bigger than my own hopes and aspirations. I was caught up in a movement with national and international implications."

Glowing with enthusiasm, she returned to Ackworth in time to make the Christmas preparations that Helen, Alice, and Bill were awaiting so eagerly.

"Well, Ruth, how did you get along?" Raymond asked.

Eyes shining, she said, "I always knew a farm wife should look beyond the fence row, but until now, I didn't realize how far you *can* see—if you'll just look!"

She went to find the small, worn hammer that fit her hand so well, intending to make a crossbar of boards for a Christmas tree stand. It was not where she usually kept it, but she spied it on the kitchen counter and said, "This is my hammer. I always *hope* to find it in the tool drawer. Who would think that anybody would take a thing like that?"

Raymond grinned. "Who else would care whether anybody took a thing like that?"

The hammer dialog was repeated so frequently that it became a family joke. The children would giggle as soon as their mother said, "This is my hammer."

That hammer was essential to the slow but sure refurbishing of the Ackworth farmhouse that began when Ruth made a new pair of bedroom curtains. The curtains made the rest of the room look shabby, so she painted it, and one thing led to another.

Remembering Mrs. Sewell's eloquence in Boston, Ruth began to think through a speech on the subject of home improvement: "The spirit of the home should flow into the community. Everyone can get a lift from people who take pride in their homes and yards. . . ." That sounded fine, she thought, or did it? She would ask Raymond.

He looked up from the *Warren County News* and listened, pursing his lips thoughtfully.

"Well, how is it?"

"There's nothing wrong with it, Ruth, but why don't you tell a funny story first to get them in a good mood?"

"Because I don't know any funny stories!"

"Something will turn up."

She left him to go and sweep the back porch. According to Raymond, the surest sign of a good housekeeper was a neat back porch, and yet he was the one who messed it up. There was his coat lying on the floor! On impulse, she returned to the kitchen, snatched the hammer from its rightful place in the tool drawer, and nailed the coat to the porch floor. Then she tried to keep a straight face while she waited for him to pick up the coat on his way to the barn.

At last he was ready to begin the chores, and she stood in the door to watch his reaction. He stooped, pulled, frowned, and finally realized what she had done. Chuckling, he gave the coat a sharp tug, ripping it from the nail. "Maybe you taught me a lesson, but it cost you something. Now you have to mend the coat!"

"It's worth it," she said, "now I have a funny story!"

As spring came on, Raymond filled Bill's coaster wagon with lambs and brought them to the house for Ruth's inspection. As she stroked the woolly babies, she considered the joys of farm living: new life, a wonderful view from every room in the house, and all kinds of breathing space.

Helen and Alice were wrapped up in 4-H work, preparing to represent the Polly Prim Club with a flower-arranging demonstration at the next Warren County Fair. They made an attractive pair in their blue middy uniforms with skirts pressed into knife-sharp pleats. Soon Bill would be old enough to show Hampshire lambs at the fair.

In 1931 Ruth Sayre attended a conference on home building and home ownership in Washington, D.C., at the invitation of President Herbert Hoover. She supported Hoover because she was a Republican, and she said, "Raymond went out to speak for him, but it didn't do any good. I felt bad when he didn't get reelected."

Although the county contact meetings for sharing Farm Bureau information were not primarily social occasions, they always included a potluck luncheon of rich food, which Ruth Sayre enjoyed. As a result, the clothes from her trousseau with their simple lines and quality material that could have been altered to last forever became too tight. But even with a drastically diminished wardrobe, Ruth Sayre managed to look well when she appeared in public.

She said, "I had two dresses with jackets that I wore to speak at ordinary meetings in the county, one blue and one taupe."

Years later, Laura Lane, a reporter for *Country Gentlewoman* and later the *Farm Journal,* was to say, "Mrs. Sayre had little time for shopping, and clothes per se were not of consuming interest to her. Good grooming was part of her secret of always looking just right for the occasion."

In the spring of 1932 the Sayres read of the organizational meeting of the Farmers Holiday Association to be held at the Iowa State Fair Grounds May 3. The leader of this effort was Milo Reno, a Populist seasoned with Campbellite theology who had the ear of many distressed farmers. Reno spoke of organized refusal to deliver the products of the farm for prices that were less than production costs. He was talking about a farmers' strike.

The Sayres knew how Reno's supporters felt, because they were suffering from the same circumstances, but they were suspicious of the presence of Harold Ware, Ella Reeve Bloor known as "Mother Bloor," and Lem Harris, who were members of the American Communist Party sent to the Midwest to create an agrarian wing of the proletarian movement.

Radical measures were uncongenial to the Sayres, and Reno's Farmers Union made them uneasy, as the Tipton Cow War had done in 1931. Late that winter a drive to eradicate bovine tuberculosis coincided with bank failures, rousing dairy farmers near Tipton, Iowa, to violence when state veterinarians came to inoculate their cattle and confiscate those that were diseased for what the owners considered to be inadequate compensation. The enraged farmers threatened state officials with guns and put sugar in their gas tanks, prompting the posting of three regiments of the Iowa National Guard to the Cedar County Fair Grounds at Tipton, which was known as Camp Bovine for the duration of the incidents. The moderate view of the Farm Bureau rejected such extreme approaches to farm problems, and, as Ruth Sayre said, "We didn't work that way."

Conditions were grim in town, too, and William Buxton, Jr., tightened his lips when the talk turned to business. His bank, Peoples Trust and Savings, had been operating for just thirteen years, and he had no intention of letting it go under in the worst financial crisis the nation had known. Because of his foresight and shrewdness, Peoples Trust and Savings was the only bank in Indianola to survive the Depression.

One cause for rejoicing in that dreary year was the installation of a furnace in the Ackworth farmhouse. No more coming home to a cold house!

In 1933 Ruth Sayre's powers of persuasion were well recognized, and she was delegated to approach Charles E. Hearst, president of the Iowa Farm Bureau, and his board to ask that the state chairman of the Iowa Farm Bureau Women be given a vote on the state Farm Bureau board rather than attend its meetings in an advisory capacity. Her plea to carry the partnership of the farmer and his wife beyond the farm was successful.

Years later she said, "If any contribution I made to the Farm Bureau was important, it was making the women an integral part of the organization. The whole point of the Farm Bureau in the beginning was to give farmers a voice, and I believed that I had helped women share in that voice. In the pioneer tradition of Iowa, women were always partners on the farm, helping with the farm work when they were needed. Why shouldn't they be partners in the Farm Bureau? I was pleased when women were released from their water-tight compartment and allowed to become involved in the whole Farm Bureau program, because that was the Iowa way."

Early in 1934 Ruth Sayre discovered that she was pregnant. She would be 38 years old when the baby was born, which put her in the high-risk range, but she was not too worried about that, and she had no intention of slacking in her Farm Bureau work.

"I had to go on with state Farm Bureau work," she said, "and I had ten counties in my district to take care of. However, the baby was due in August, and there weren't too many meetings in the summer. I did take a few months off."

John Sayre was born in the Indianola hospital, delivered by Dr. Ernest Shaw.

By now running water was one of the amenities of the Ackworth household, which was a boon for the mother of an infant, and the other children were old enough to be of help. They realized that it would be some time before they regained the freedom of the days when the whole family participated in the girls' Home Management demonstration that won first place at county and state fairs, earning them an unforgettable trip to the International Club Congress in Chicago.

Impressed by Farm Bureau support of the Triple A Act of 1933, which President Ed O'Neal labeled "Magna Carta of agriculture," Raymond Sayre consented to serve as Warren County's first Triple A chairman. The act, which was designed to limit production, was based on voluntary participation and was to be administered by local and county committees, and it seemed a possible answer to the surpluses that were driving prices down. Something had to be done.

Nature had a way of limiting production too. After the severe drought of 1934, the Sayres did not pick one ear of corn on their farm. Mrs. Sayre said, "Anyone who lived through those times was permanently marked. They could never again spend a dollar with wild abandon."

In 1935 the Associated Women of the American Farm Bureau joined the Associated Country Women of the World, much to Ruth Sayre's delight, and when she heard that Grace Frysinger had arranged for the third Triennial to be held in Washington, D.C., in 1936, she was determined to go. That anticipation and her busy schedule in District Eight would get her through the rigorous winter of 1936 and the earth-baking drought that followed it.

V. B. Hamilton said, "I remember Ruth Sayre working her counties soon after John was born, taking him with her in a basket in the back of the old Ford."

Now, John was too active to be transported in a basket, and he spent a great deal of time with Anna Buxton, having a wonderful time with "Mamma." That is where he was on the frigid morning of February 5, 1936, when his mother and Mrs. H. H. Beebe of Council Bluffs were the only Master Farm Homemakers hardy enough to make it to Ames on time for a meeting of the guild. The severity of that winter is legendary.

The 1936 Triennial of the Associated Country Women of the World in Washington, D.C., drew 200 delegates, and nearly 7,000 American farm women came to the nation's capital by the trainload to attend the conference. Ruth Sayre was among them.

Although she had seen the sights of the conference city with her mother years before, many of the farm wives were making their first trip to Washington, and they regarded it as a lark, crowding the streets and thronging to the tourist attractions as excited as young girls. Washingtonians never had seen so many farm women all at once.

Some of the women had formed state groups on the trains enroute to the meeting, and groups previously organized had arranged sessions in Washington, drawing on a pool of international talent for their programs.

Ruth Sayre, who was now president of the Master Farm Homemakers Guild, represented that body on the conference committee and had done her homework to chair a discussion of country women and the economic problem. Her interest in economics did not stem from love of the subject. The girl who wanted to abolish grade school arithmetic had become the woman who saw the need for translating profit and loss or supply and demand into bread and butter realities.

The Master Farm Homemakers Guild met to hear Fru Michelet of Norway describe the aims of the Associated Country Women of the World: to promote and maintain friendly, helpful relations; to further the common interests of member organizations; and to encourage the formation of women's organizations in countries where that need had not been met. The Norwegian delegate told of the London headquarters of ACWW, a suite of small, dark rooms at the top of a winding stair known as "old Number 78," and Ruth Sayre hoped that someday she might visit that shrine. The hope seemed quite remote, however.

Eleanor Roosevelt, the First Lady of the land, invited all the women attending the conference to tea at the White House, and when they came by the thousands, spilling over the grounds, aides were sent scurrying to borrow enough teacups to serve them.

President Franklin D. Roosevelt spoke to the gathering, as did Henry A. Wallace, secretary of agriculture. Some of the women were breathless with awe, and Ruth Sayre shared their feeling about the president, but she had known Secretary Wallace as an editor of *Wallaces' Farmer* and had heard him speak at an Iowa Farm bureau meeting. Also, she thought, smiling to herself, she had known Wallace's wife better than she cared to at one time—when she was Ilo

Browne and practiced the piano all too diligently within Anna Buxton's hearing. Still another factor made Henry A. Wallace seem less than formidable. His mother was a Pi Phi.

Although Ruth Sayre was a Republican through and through, she always gave credit to a Democrat when credit was due. Years later, she said of Wallace, "I thought he was an able administrator."

7

Madam Chairman

IN 1937, the year Helen entered Simpson College, her mother became chairman of the Iowa Farm Bureau Women. V. B. Hamilton said, "I don't think Ruth Sayre ever ran for an office. They always asked her to serve."

When Hamilton came to the Iowa Farm Bureau in 1935, Mrs. Ellsworth Richardson was chairman, and he described her as "an evangelist." Roger Fleming says, "Mrs. Sayre had to follow a person who had established a national reputation as a leader, and I'm confident that she did not want a comparison to reflect adversely on her. It never did."

Ruth Sayre admitted, "The executive sessions were long and tiring for me at first. I had had no training in business administration and learned it the hard way."

She learned quickly, however, and set about reorganizing the Iowa Farm Bureau Women. They had no budget of their own, making special requests to fund activities as they came along, and Mrs. Sayre convinced Hamilton that the women could manage their own money.

"She was down-to-earth and solid," Hamilton said, "and I told the board, 'Let's give them a lump sum and let them go on their own. Mrs. Sayre will know how to handle it.' One of the men was worried, but I told him they would do better than the men. Later on, they all admitted how beautifully the women had managed."

The budget of $3,800 was drawn up carefully, allowing $2.50 a day for a hotel room and 3½ cents a mile for travel in the line of Farm Bureau duty. The committee not only lived within its budget that first year, but $653.82 of the allotted sum remained unspent.

When Ruth Sayre assumed the state presidency of the Women's Committee, the Iowa Farm Bureau was in a state of change. V. B. Hamilton was regarded as a new broom to set the Farm Bureau house in order. He arrived to find its membership down to 20,000 and the finances in confusion. The first step was refinancing, and this was accomplished with a procedure still in use which has been copied all over the Midwest.

Hamilton said, "Mrs. Sayre was one of my best supporters, together with Allan Kline, and they both became national Farm Bureau officers. When Mrs. Sayre would take a position, I never knew a man to oppose her. She didn't do it often—mostly on principles—and she left the business end to the men. The corporations had failed, and the ones we set up to replace them are still operating successfully without changing a single rule."

The failed businesses were started in the first seventeen years of the Iowa Farm Bureau's existence when there was no separation between policymaking and administration. Hamilton explained, "Policymakers have authority to do everything, but they must have the sense not to get into the business end. Board members make policies and write resolutions, but we have to hire people who know how to do business. Separating policymaking from administration was the key."

Hamilton's suggestion of a management board to carry on day-to-day business while a resolutions committee set policy was not accepted without a fight, and Ruth Sayre and Allan Kline were on Hamilton's side. There were those who insisted that such a procedure would ruin the Farm Bureau.

"Who owns the Farm Bureau?" Hamilton asked, quickly answering his own question, "the members."

At length, the idea was approved, and a resolutions committee was set up consisting of nine district men, a woman, and the Farm Bureau vice-president in the chair without a vote. Hamilton hired a young and newly married Iowa State College graduate, Roger Fleming, to serve as secretary, also without a vote. Fleming also headed the new Research Department.

Ruth Sayre met Roger Fleming in the fall of 1938, when she approached V. B. Hamilton to ask for help with the Women's Committee work. Hamilton said, "Roger Fleming was her boy all the way through—and still is. He was her buddy, and they would leave our office saying, 'We're going over to the Kirkwood to write three chapters about Farm Bureau Women.' "

Together, Mrs. Sayre and Fleming created six pamphlets on major program areas for county leaders. The subjects were roads, schools, taxes, international trade, health, and libraries—each mimeographed on paper of a different color. Ruth Sayre asked Raymond what he thought of them, and he said nothing, but when she pressed him, he grinned and offered, "They include everything that you and Roger know in six easy lessons." According to Fleming, "He was almost right."

Fleming realized that he was "labeled as belonging to the women," but, he says, "for me, it was a badge of honor. Mrs. Sayre never asked for special privilege as the only woman on the board. She was tireless in digging out facts that would help farmers, and she always made the women understand that she knew and shared their experience."

He also notes that the idea of a queen contest came up repeatedly in meetings, "and then she would inquire as to whether better use might not be made of the time and energy that otherwise would go into the administration and promotion of such a contest. If the queen contest proposal had not been killed by then, she would return to the question of qualifications, inquiring about the relative weight to be given to brains on the one hand and measurements on the other. She never had to pursue the matter beyond this point, and she never lost a vote."

Although Raymond Sayre had been a Triple A committeeman in the honeymoon period of that agency, he and Ruth withdrew their approval when the AAA became the proverbial camel with its nose in the tent, assuming its right to speak for all farmers. The Farm Bureau took issue with this contention, stating that a free, independent organization should be the voice of agriculture rather than an agency supported by the government.

Ruth Sayre climbed into her Ford and drove to Farm Bureau meetings all over the state to warn the members that allowing the Triple A to speak for them would lodge too much power in the government and erode their own freedoms.

When Mrs. Sayre came to the board of the Iowa Farm Bureau, the president was Francis Johnson, a former Speaker of the Iowa House of Representatives. Johnson was succeeded by Allan Kline, who had earned his B.A. degree from Morningside College in Sioux City, Iowa, before his seventeenth birthday. His education included four years of Latin and four years of German.

The relationship between Kline and Ruth Sayre was one of mutual respect, and she said, "He was a shrewd economist who understood people and was willing to fight for what he thought was good for agriculture. He had known the experience of farming during the Depression, and he had the ability to think straight."

One day Kline looked at Mrs. Sayre quizzically and asked, "Don't you ever get a new winter coat?"

A self-reliant family (Bill, Alice, Raymond, and Helen) helped Ruth Sayre manage a busy schedule in 1938.

She stood straighter in the worn garment and said, "I do when I have the money."

Years later, Ruth Sayre said, "If I suggested something and Al Kline thought it was something that needed to be done, it was all right with him. We reported back, and if he had thought we were doing the wrong thing, he would have told us, but he backed us up if he thought we were doing something important."

Allan Kline's widow says, "My husband had great respect and admiration for Mrs. Sayre. He considered her tops as a public speaker and said, 'She always rang the bell,' meaning that she got her point across."

Raymond had been named a director of the Omaha Federal Land Bank and was involved with the Farm Credit Administration at the local level. Ruth Sayre said, "It wasn't as if he were in some other kind of business. We were in business together, and he was just as interested as I was in building up the Farm Bureau and making it an organization where farmers could work together."

F. W. Beckman of *The Farmer's Wife* had written to Raymond, "You are to be congratulated upon having the good judgment to pick out a wife like Mrs. Sayre." Later, Raymond was interviewed about life with his increasingly famous wife and asked how he got along when she was away so much, especially with four youngsters at home. "We always get along fine," he said, "I love to cook." Because Raymond Sayre's masculinity was unassailable, he never felt threatened by Ruth's achievements in the world beyond their home, and she said, "I have the best of all possible husbands."

With Raymond's complete support, Ruth Sayre was busy changing the direction of the Iowa Farm Bureau Women's Committee. Cheesemaking and the construction of dress forms were all very well, but she was determined to persuade the women to use their heads as well as their hands. In the speeches that became as natural to her as breathing, she said, "If you don't use your brains, like any muscle, they will wither away."

At first, the brain work she advocated was directed toward making the organization more businesslike. Written minutes and a budget were adopted, and the committee meeting became a training school taught by specialists and members of the state Farm Bureau staff before the members went out into the counties to pass the information along. The six colored pamphlets, "all we know in six easy lessons," were used and distributed at county contact meetings.

The women tackled problems in areas of greatest need, and with the scarcity of medical and hospital services for rural people in the late 1930s, a health program was high on their priority list. In 1938 the women recommended that the Farm Bureau sponsor Blue Cross Health Insurance, but it would be more than three decades (1970) before their suggestion was acted upon.

In great demand as a speaker, Ruth Sayre traveled all over the country to address conventions and farm institutes. John Sayre remembers hearing his mother speak in his preschool days, and he says, "Sometimes I went along if it wasn't too far, and I would have to sit in the back of the room because I was restless and bored with an adult meeting."

Judging from the letters that came to his mother after a speaking engagement, John's youthful reaction was unique. A Kentucky woman wrote, "You come into my kitchen days when I iron or bake, and I hear you speak of your vision in my kitchen."

Edith Barker, a state 4-H Club leader, wrote, "You brought humanity, understanding, and a very deep challenge"; and Bess Newcomer of Moulton, Iowa, referred to Ruth Sayre as "One who earns her honors so honestly," saying, "some of your success must lie in your painstaking care of details."

From Alicia Olson of Brookings, South Dakota, came a letter that read, "I have been thinking and thinking about the talk you gave the farm women here on Thursday and wishing that every homemaker in South Dakota might have heard it. It was so practical and inspirational."

Many letters contained wistful statements like, "I had hoped to talk with you at the convention, but too many other people were crowded around you."

Following Ruth Sayre's 1937 dinner address in New York City, May Bevens, chairman of the Committee on Urban-Rural Cooperation, wrote, "A lovely address: sound, interesting, well-arranged, and well thought through."

Mrs. Sayre spoke at a Farm Bureau picnic in Iowa City; a Rural Home Conference in Kansas; an Institute of Rural Affairs in Virginia; a rural young people's camp in Iowa; and at the annual meeting of the Grocers' Wholesale Corporation, Inc., in Des Moines, where she said, "I don't understand why grocers don't see to it that a spice can is developed permitting the housewife to use a teaspoon to dispense the contents as well as a shaker top." The grocers assured her that such an improvement was in the works.

V. B. Hamilton said, "She wasn't an orator, but she could handle sentence structure, and when she spoke at a district conference in Kansas City, they stood and cheered."

Roger Fleming recalls, "In public speeches, Mrs. Sayre quickly established a common link with her audience, usually by saying something that proved beyond the question of a doubt that she had shared or was sharing experiences they had encountered. She drove throughout the state in all kinds of weather and on all kinds of roads successfully importuning farm women to become active in a voluntary organization like the Farm Bureau."

Reconsidering his childhood reaction to his mother's speeches, John Sayre says, "They *were* forceful."

Ruth Sayre said, "I depended very much on Raymond for ideas and for bolstering my own ideas. I read all my planned speeches to him, wanting his opinion especially if I suspected I had gone a little haywire on an idea or overdramatized something, as women will do. But I felt what I said. It wasn't just a speech, I was trying to put across something I believed in." She added with a wry laugh, "Most of the time they took it, but sometimes they didn't."

Opal Swarthout, the Ackworth postmistress, marveled at the influx of letters addressed to Mrs. Sayre. They included a plea from a woman who wanted to buy the farm she was living on so that she and her mother could have a home. The woman had no money, and she asked Ruth Sayre to collect five cents from each woman in the Farm Bureau for her cause.

One thing that Ruth Sayre never learned was the use of the typewriter. She hired young typists from Indianola to come to the farm and help her work through the stacks of correspondence that covered the dining room table, dictating some letters and writing others in her own neat hand if the young women did not take shorthand.

A friend she had made in 1936, Gertrude Dieken, who was then home economics editor for the Extension Service at Iowa State College, would become Woman's Editor of the *Farm Journal* and work closely with Ruth Sayre on numerous articles for that magazine. Mrs. Sayre's writing also would appear in *Successful Farming, Women's Press,* and the *American Home Economics Journal,* but Gertrude Dieken was responsible for her closest relationship with the world of publishing. They lunched for business and pleasure and appeared on panels together.

In 1938 Ruth Sayre was occupied with a new responsibility as Midwest Regional Director of the Associated Women of the American Farm Bureau Federation, a job that she juggled with her state chairmanship in Iowa.

As V. B. Hamilton put it, "They came after her. She didn't run for the office. In Chicago they saw how she could fight for the principles we had set up in Iowa. She had an awful time with some of those women trying to convince them that when a bank president puts a son not worth a lead nickel in an important position, that is not separation of policy and business."

The Associated Women provided an umbrella for women connected with state Farm Bureaus and groups that had no such connection like the Illinois and New York Home Bureaus. The Associated Women of the AFBF elected their own officers and adopted their own resolutions and programs but were financed by the AFBF, and their president had a vote on the AFBF board.

Ruth Sayre was now a member of the national women's board, one of four regional directors elected by delegates from the states. The experience opened her eyes to the differences in agricultural interests in the United States. Her own midwestern viewpoint was stretched to include a concern for the farm problems of the East, West, and South, and she finally saw American agriculture as a whole.

Her duties as Midwest director included two to four board meetings a year, the Midwest Training School for Farm Bureau Leaders (men and women), and three or four state annual meetings. If this had been her only job, she could have managed it with one hand tied behind her back, but she also had urgent business in Iowa.

Farm Bureau women in Iowa had chosen a project to encourage reading. If they were to deal with current issues intelligently, they needed books for study, and they also needed books for recreation. The problem was the lack of library service to rural areas, and the Farm Bureau women were working for legislation to extend such service to farm families.

Accompanied by several members of the Women's Committee, Ruth Sayre took to the floor of the Iowa House of Representatives to campaign for rural library legislation. The *Des Moines Register* reported, "The men argued back that they feared to push the measure, but Mrs. Sayre insisted even more emphatically, until the men backed down and voted to get behind the drive for rural libraries."

As a clincher, Ruth Sayre led her delegation into the office of Governor George A. Wilson to plead for the library bill. "It was the first time we had called on a governor," she said, "and it didn't work. Governor Wilson refused to support the bill, and it lost in the later administration of Governor Robert Blue."

Roger Fleming recalls, "We got clobbered, and as Mrs. Sayre and I were sitting in the Capitol cafeteria drinking milk and licking our wounds, she said, 'Hundreds of dollars for manure, but not one cent for literature! When I think of all the time I spent lobbying for that bill . . . ! ' "

Ironically, it was during the 1938 fight for library legislation that Ruth Sayre noticed she was having trouble with her eyes. Glasses were prescribed, and she said, "I knew I had to have them, but I didn't like it very much."

The Associated Women of the American Farm Bureau Federation also were working for a bill to extend library services to rural areas, and Ruth knew that its day would come. Another issue important at state and national levels was funding for the educational work of the Extension Service, the brightest and best hope for bringing farm women into the twentieth century as far as advantages and opportunities were concerned.

Ruth Sayre's tiny engagement book was neatly crammed with entries, and she managed to meet her many obligations with the help of a kitchen blackboard. Under the heading "Who wants the car?" the family signed up, "7–11, Daddy. 3:30, Mother. 7:30, Alice." Under "Today's Schedule," Alice wrote her dental appointment beneath Helen's meeting. "Week's Plan" listed this ambitious schedule: "Monday—wash, clean basement. Tuesday—iron, mend.

When Mrs. Sayre was able to stay at home in 1938,
she enjoyed feeding her family well.

Wednesday—bake, clean cupboards. Thursday—clean, Ladies Aid. Friday—dust books, clean bookcases. Saturday—bake, clean kitchen.'' Sunday, the day of rest, was unscheduled. Everyone in the family knew that the first priority was church.

On a particularly busy day, John Sayre recalls, his mother would dash into the kitchen early in the morning singing, "I have bread to bake and beer to brew, and what, oh what am I to do?" Not exactly a Methodist ditty, this was an effective work song.

Ruth Sayre had been initiated into her mother's chapter of the PEO Sisterhood, BP, but she was too busy with farm affairs to attend many chapter meetings in her younger years. The association would take on more meaning later in her life.

As a college girl, Helen Sayre was a beauty with a special glow about her, and John, then a preschooler, remembers, "She had lots of boyfriends." Talking together late one night, Ruth and Raymond marveled at the swift flight of time since the winter day when they brought Helen home from the hospital to the cold farmhouse at New Virginia. Many of those fast-moving years had been hard, but things were better now. Both Helen and Alice were at Simpson, and Ruth even had a new winter coat.

8

Another War

EARLY in 1939 the atmosphere was heavy with rumors of war, but Ruth Buxton Sayre's natural optimism asserted itself as she made arrangements for her first trip abroad. The fourth Triennial of the Associated Country Women of the World was to be held in London.

As she applied for a passport and accommodations on the *Queen Mary*, she scarcely could believe that the pictures in her mother's travel magazines soon would come to life for her—that she actually would visit Grandpa Buxton's homeland.

Ruth Sayre was accustomed to domestic travel and said, "I always had a case almost packed and knew what had to go into it," but a protracted trip overseas called for more intense preparation. After crossing the ocean for the conference, she meant to see at least a little more of Europe before coming home.

Before the *Queen Mary* sailed, Mrs. Sayre made a radio broadcast from the New York World's Fair, expressing her hopes for international cooperation among country women.

Greatly excited by the glamor of the great ocean liner's departure, Ruth Sayre stood at the rail until the New York skyline vanished. When she could see nothing but sea and sky, she was assailed by an uneasiness that soon turned to seasickness. She said, "I spent a good deal of time in a chair on the deck. Fresh air seemed to help."

In London the expectation of war was dramatically evident. Bomb shelters were being dug in Hyde Park, and at the Triennial sessions, German women substituted the clenched fist salute and the cry of "Heil Hitler!" for applause.

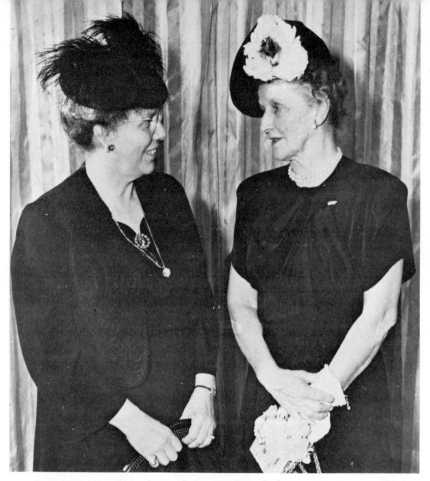

On her first trip abroad, Ruth Sayre visited the
country home of Lady Nancy Astor, and the
women were friends for years, as evidenced by this
photograph from a National Farm Institute
meeting in Des Moines.

The delegates climbed the winding stairs to "old Number 78" to visit the heart of ACWW and were impressed by the strength of rural women's organizations upheld by the patronage of the English nobility. They were entertained at Goldsmith Hall, Marlborough House, and Cliveden, the beautiful home of Lady Nancy Astor, who was to become an ardent admirer of Ruth Buxton Sayre, with the admiration mutual.

Visiting the Tower of London, Westminster Abbey, and the Houses of Parliament, Ruth Sayre had a sense of homecoming. She thrilled to the pomp and pageantry of the trooping of the colors to celebrate the birthday of King George VI and admired the young

Princesses Elizabeth and Margaret, but democracy was so deeply instilled in her being that she regarded the Windsors as humans, however royal. Through the years, she was to be as much at ease with a queen as with a farm wife in Warren County.

At the end of the Triennial, Mrs. Sayre joined a tour of Scandinavia organized for Farm Bureau women, talking with country women in Norway, Sweden, and Denmark through an interpreter. Their goals were like hers: to rear a family well and to achieve a reasonable return for their labor. Women were women, whatever their land or language.

When most of the American women went home, Ruth Sayre persuaded a friend from California to accompany her to the continent. Her aunt, Ida Reynolds, had given her money to make at least a stab at the Grand Tour, and the two women went by train to Milan, enjoying the dreamlike beauty of Lago Maggiore and Lucerne on the way. They continued on to Paris, where Ruth found her college French to be rusty but serviceable enough to find Notre Dame, the Louvre, and the tomb of Napoleon. After all, she thought, she might never have another opportunity to see the sights of Europe.

She returned home with a kaleidoscope of memories: the polyglot delegates at the Triennial and the redoubtable Mrs. Alfred Watt at the helm; a farm wife making goat cheese in Norway; the beauty of the Alps; the fields of Italy, more beautiful to an artist than to a farmer; the imposing monuments of London and Paris; and a deep uneasiness about the harbingers of war.

When Hitler's forces invaded Czechoslovakia in September 1939, making war a reality, the Extension Service at Cornell University at Ithaca, New York, swiftly issued an invitation to the Associated Country Women of the World to move the headquarters from war-threatened London to the Cornell campus. The move was discussed vigorously, even heatedly, and in the end, the headquarters remained in London. Ruth Sayre agreed with the decision, considering England to be the organization's home and the mother country of many of its members. Also, she did not believe that the United States had arrived at a world view wide enough to make this country an effective base for the international organization.

Arriving at that conclusion caused her to formulate her first thoughts on the "international mind," and later she would say, "The national mind is enclosed all around by the borders of its country. The international mind knows that a threat to peace and freedom in any part of the world is a threat to peace and freedom in all parts of the world."

The fall of 1940 saw Alice transferring to the State University of

Iowa in Iowa City to pursue her political science studies. Helen had remained at home while attending college, so Alice was the first bird to fly from the nest.

In 1940 Ruth Sayre was elected president of the American Country Life Association and was the first farm woman to hold the position. The association, which was founded after President Theodore Roosevelt's Country Life Commission's report stirred new interest and concern for rural living in America, held an annual meeting at Purdue University. Presiding over that meeting and delivering a presidential address were Mrs. Sayre's chief duties in the office.

She represented the American Country Life Association at the Fortune Round Table in Atlantic City in mid-April 1940, participating in a panel on agriculture with university professors and board chairmen from companies like Montgomery Ward, General Mills, Hormel, Armour, Safeway, and R. J. Reynolds. The theme of the round table was the social importance of sound agriculture to American democracy, and the discussion covered distribution of government subsidies, improvement of soil conservation, questions of government control, problems of tenancy and farm rehabilitation, markets, freight rates, and the cost of farm implements. At this meeting, what Roger Fleming calls Mrs. Sayre's "almost insatiable interest in obtaining factual information useful to farmers" paid off.

A highlight of 1940 was the Women's Centennial Congress in New York City, which reviewed the progress of American women in the century past and attempted to plot a course for the future. Ruth Sayre participated in a panel discussion of the problems of the 1940 woman with Margaret Mead, anthropologist, and Pearl Buck, novelist. Eleanor Roosevelt was the moderator, and Mrs. Sayre said, "Her knowledge and understanding of the problems of rural women made my participation easy and effective." A large audience of urban women listened intently to "the voice of the farm."

Attending the American Farm Bureau Federation's annual meeting at the Lord Baltimore Hotel in Baltimore, Maryland, in mid-December, Ruth Sayre discussed the problems of nutrition for defense with other delegates.

As she prepared for the holidays, Ruth Sayre reviewed her year, noting that it had brought a special sadness in the death of Aunt Ida, Anna Buxton's sister, on July 14.

Helen's graduation from Simpson College in June 1941 filled the Sayres with great pride and satisfaction, and when she left for the East to begin graduate studies at New York University, they congratulated themselves on beating the "can't have it" attitude one more time.

That same month Ruth Sayre attended the national meeting of the

A special family closeness is seen in this photograph of the early 1940s of Raymond, Bill, Helen, Alice, John, and Ruth Sayre.

American Library Association in Boston, and she returned to give speeches on books for rural homes and schools in Wisconsin and Minnesota. On this subject, the Master Farm Homemakers had been ahead of their time, promoting rural library service since 1931. The Guild also urged efforts to secure world peace before anyone dreamed that a second worldwide conflict could be possible.

At Eleanor Roosevelt's suggestion, Mrs. Sayre was appointed to New York Mayor Fiorello LaGuardia's Civilian Defense Committee, which was launched with a luncheon at the White House on July 24, 1941. The farm wife from Ackworth, Iowa, had moved from the White House lawn to its dining room, and *Life* magazine covered the event.

LaGuardia told the committee, "People in this country unfortunately haven't got enough idea of what modern war means." Adept at the art of plain talk, he said, "About the question of politics, somebody may start it. Don't bring it to me. You are Americans, and you don't belong to any party in this work."

Mrs. Sayre said of LaGuardia, "He was outgoing and enthusiastic. I don't recall that I had any differences with him, because we both were trying to do something to save people's lives. He talked a lot and assumed he had a lot of power, which he did, compared to what I had."

The war in Europe was heating up, and the ACWW office in London was bombed out of several buildings, finally settling in the flat of one of the members. Mrs. Watt moved back to Canada for the duration, and she called a regional conference of American and Canadian women in September 1941.

Princess Julianna of the Netherlands also had taken refuge in Canada during the war, and Mrs. Watt invited her to participate in the regional conference. As one of the speakers on the program, Ruth Sayre found herself first in line to be introduced to the Dutch princess.

Mrs. Sayre said, "I wondered if I should curtsey or shake hands. Whatever I did would be repeated by those who came after me, and making the correct choice was up to me. I still hadn't made up my mind by the time Mrs. Watt said, 'Your Highness, this is Mrs. Ruth Sayre from Ackworth, Iowa,' but the princess solved the problem by extending her hand."

The purpose of the conference was to map out a plan for postwar reconstruction, looking forward to peace while the governments of the world still were preoccupied with war.

Speaking on the last day of the conference, Ruth Sayre said, "It is vital to the future that women not only be informed, but that they be prepared to take full responsibility. Every time we speak of a right, we must speak of a responsibility."

Knowing that there could be no Triennial while the war lasted, the members realized the importance of working for peace wherever they were. Mrs. Watt closed the conference on a hopeful note, saying, "We will not forget the noble appeal of Mrs. Sayre."

Less than three months later the Japanese attacked Pearl Harbor and the United States was at war. Ruth Sayre learned of the attack at the 1941 Farm Bureau convention, where Oveta Culp Hobby, the chief officer of the Women's Army Corps, made the announcement to the audience gathered for the first night's general session. Like everyone around her, she felt shock and a sense of dread about what was to come.

A letter from Fiorello LaGuardia dated December 13, 1941, urged Ruth Sayre to "keep calm and unafraid," which was easier said than done, but she did keep busy with war bond campaigns, the Advisory Committee of the War Savings Staff, the Civilian Defense Advisory Committee, and the Women's Division of the Iowa Salvage Section of the War Production Chest Committee. She also was involved in making mattresses for the needy from surplus cotton from the south.

Ruth Sayre planted a larger home garden to help the war effort, and it seemed likely that she would have to help with the farm work when it became impossible to get a hired man. All the young men in the county were rushing to the armed services.

The war became extremely personal to the Sayres in 1942, when 18-year-old Bill enlisted in the Marine Corps and was sent to San Diego for training.

Mrs. Sayre said, "The day he left, I went to Ames to give a talk for a group of housemothers. It filled a difficult day for me."

John Sayre remembers, "When my parents heard that Bill was to be sent overseas, they made a quick decision. Dad was at a meeting in Muscatine, but Mother picked me up at school and announced that we were leaving for California that afternoon. What fun!

"When we arrived in Kansas City, we had no further train reservations on to Los Angeles, and there was no place to sit but in the ladies' rest room. Mother and I were there until Dad got reservations for the rest of the trip. When we finally got there, we stayed with Mother's cousin, Grace Cooper Hardy, and her family, and when Bill had to go back to Camp Pendleton, we said good-bye to him at the corner of Hollywood and Vine and continued on home—this time with train reservations."

Letters from Bill arrived from the Solomon Islands, then Okinawa, and Ruth Sayre worried about her Marine son, who in a peacetime world would have been a freshman at Iowa State College.

In her speeches of that time, Mrs. Sayre stressed the duty of each generation to do its part in keeping America's hard-won freedom. She had a "B" gas rationing card and prayed that the supply in her tank would last between open gas stations; also that the car would hold up until the unforeseeable time when they could get a new one. On her more distant journeys, she had to contend with crowded railroad stations and cars, and the schedules were uncertain. Many times she sat up all night in a coach seat between Washington, D.C., and Chicago.

Simpson College, Ruth Buxton Sayre's alma mater, awarded her an honorary Doctor of Laws degree on the twenty-fifth anniversary of her graduation in June 1942. The graduating class that day was predominantly female with so many young men at war.

The Sayres also attended Alice's commencement exercises at the State University of Iowa and talked over her plans for graduate study at Harvard. Helen had completed her studies at New York University and planned to teach at Ankeny, near Des Moines, in the fall.

During the war years one of the main thrusts of the Iowa Farm Bureau was school reorganization. Ruth Sayre embraced the issue wholeheartedly, believing that she should try to complete the unfinished business of her great grandfather, Dr. William Reynolds. As Iowa's first superintendent of public instruction in 1841, Dr. Reynolds had reported a plan "to effect an immediate organization of the primary school system in Iowa," placing school houses at two-mile intervals. The state legislature not only deemed the project too expensive, but it legislated Dr. Reynolds' office out of existence. Reynolds did, however, accomplish one goal—the establishment of a state school fund.

Iowa Governor Bourke B. Hickenlooper appointed Ruth Sayre to the School Code Commission in 1943, and she was the sole woman and the only rural person on the commission.

The Iowa Farm Bureau Women's Committee had long supported by resolution the reorganization of rural schools and more state aid for education. Now it was time to go beyond the resolution stage. The problems were great. Iowa was near the bottom of the national list in state aid to schools, and local property tax bore nearly 100 percent of the school tax load. The system created the inequity of farmers paying $142 per year for each school child while town dwellers paid only $37 for the same services. Statistics showed that rural teachers, eighty-three percent of them with a year of college or less, were paid $622 a year. Out of 100 rural children, only 43 went on to high school. Four of that hundred went to college, but only 1 graduated.

Remembering her own teaching experience, Ruth Sayre was determined to improve rural education. Many country school pupils would leave the farm, and they would need an education adequate for becoming part of a town business community. Those who stayed on the farm would need an education that prepared them to cope with the new technology in farming.

To sell the reorganization idea, the Farm Bureau set up a series of district meetings in March 1943. Ruth Sayre and Professor J. A. Starrak, who taught vocational education at Iowa State College, spoke at the meetings, outlining the problems and proposals of the Code Commission and answering questions.

Important as the education issue was, a family matter took precedence over it that March. Helen was engaged to Richard Jacobs, a Simpson College classmate who lived on a neighboring farm. A member of the Army Air Corps, Dick Jacobs had just earned his wings and had asked Helen to come to Colorado and marry him.

Remembering her own wartime wedding, Ruth Sayre regretted that Helen could not be married at home, but she managed to get herself, her mother, and John on a troop train headed west and arrived in time for the March 10 ceremony in the Methodist church at La Junta, Colorado, where Alice joined them.

Helen was a beautiful bride in a blue tailored suit adorned by Dick's wings and a corsage of red roses. The newlyweds began life together in Colorado, and then Helen followed her husband to Clovis, New Mexico. When Dick was sent to the South Pacific, she came home to Ackworth to await his return.

Ruth Sayre resumed the district meetings with J. A. Starrak, informing Farm Bureau school committees of both men and women and the county and township women's school chairmen, who were to carry the facts to their own districts. Counties surveyed their schools and compared results, learning the true state of education in home territory. Farm people discovered that they were paying a higher price than their town neighbors for an education inferior to that of nonrural pupils.

Mrs. Sayre made radio broadcasts, wrote letters, and spoke in all parts of the state about the need for equal educational opportunity for rural children and better training for rural school teachers. Repeatedly she said, "One-room country schools are relics of horse-and-buggy days and do not meet modern needs. They cannot prepare rural children, many of whom will leave the farm, for the larger, complex world in which they will live."

Wherever country people gathered, they enjoyed good food with their fellowship, and Ruth Sayre took as much pleasure in eating as any of them. She particularly loved chocolate pie. However, she had been noticing the pangs of indigestion more and more frequently. When she came home from a meeting one night, the pain was acute, and Helen said, "Mother, is something wrong? You don't look well."

Buxton that she was, Ruth Sayre managed a smile and said, "Oh, it was just something I ate. It will be all right."

Raymond, who knew all about his wife's stoicism, insisted that she see a doctor, and the diagnosis was gallstones. An operation was indicated, but Ruth protested that she was much too busy with school reorganization to consider surgery. When the family continued to insist, she entered the hospital that hot July "to get it over with!"

She made a good recovery, aided by a flood of letters and get-well cards from friends and admirers. Marian Inman of Bancroft, Iowa, wrote, "I've thought of you all these hot days when I've been steaming along. Canned peas and cherries, got all the weeds out of the garden. I had my choice this past hour of mending overalls or writing letters. The overalls are still there."

Other letters mentioned the burned-out lawns and the terrible heat, but they all encouraged Ruth Sayre to leave her hospital bed and go on speaking for them, saying that she knew what was on their minds. Before she was dismissed from the hospital, a heavy sorrow fell upon the whole family.

Nine-year-old John was home alone with Helen when the call came on the party line. Dick Jacobs was missing in action in the South Pacific.

Roger Fleming has referred to Ruth Sayre's courage in adversity, saying, "Mrs. Sayre is a strong person, and there are far too few of them around these days." She summoned that strength in the difficult days of mid-July 1943.

Adding to a Master Farm Homemaker round robin in early August, she wrote, "The letter reached me in the hospital, where I was recovering from an operation, hence I am a little slow in answering. Don't know why anyone goes to the hospital in July, but I needed to have my gallbladder out and thought I'd better get it over.

"I worked in the garden the day before I went to the hospital and got out every weed, but the family has had to take over since then. We have put a lot of food in the locker and are canning apricots this week.

"My oldest daughter, Helen, has been at home helping me since the middle of June, when her husband went overseas. Everything here has been overshadowed by the news she had last week that her husband had been missing in action since July 13 in the South Pacific. We hope that he (as many others have) will be found safe and well, but it takes lots of courage and faith to face these days.

"Alice received her M.A. at Harvard this spring and is in Washington, D.C., working in the State Department. She has done special work in this field. William has been helping his father with the farm work this summer. The crops are better than it looked like they would be earlier. Only the hay crop is really short. My small John is growing up and has learned to take a lot of responsibility this summer.

"I have been doing a lot of reading—Lippman's *U.S. Foreign Policy, Preface to Peace,* a symposium. I'm now reading *Head-Hunting in the Solomons.* Sounds terrible but is most interesting. Don't expect to take on any outside activities before September. I'm really going to have a vacation. Besides, my family is due a 'priority rating!' "

All hope for Dick Jacobs's survival vanished when his personal belongings were returned to Helen. Widowed so soon after becoming a wife, Helen decided to help other servicemen, and because her sister Alice was living in Washington, D.C., she chose to go there and work for the USO.

Moved by her daughter's grief, Ruth Sayre was more determined than ever to fight for the cause of world peace, but first she must deal with the necessities of war, representing farm women on the National Committee for the Protection of Children in Wartime, the Women's Interest Section of the War Department, and the regional Office of Civilian Defense.

The wartime Christmas of 1943 was further flawed by Helen's loss and Bill's absence, but it was memorable in its own way. Ruth's father had surprised the family with the announcement that he always had coveted a diamond ring, a desire seemingly out of keeping with his conservative nature. When the gifts were opened, he received not one, but two diamond rings—one from John Scott, the husband of Ruth's sister Martha, and the other from a friend, the Reverend Walter C. Plank. Both were of the finest glass, and William Buxton, Jr., enjoyed the joke hugely.

The day after Christmas, Ruth's father suffered a slight stroke, and as soon as it was possible, her brother Bill would arrange for release from his duties as a Navy flight instructor at Pensacola to come home and take over the bank.

9

Picking up the Pieces

IN 1944 Ruth Sayre became vice-president of the American Farm Bureau Federation Women, which meant more meetings, and she pursued the goals of the Associated Women with even more vigor. The long fight for a truth-in-fabrics bill was continued, and the women pressed for a bill extending library service to rural areas, appropriations for the Extension Service, and the Hill-Burton hospital bill for improving health services to rural people.

At this time, the Associated Women of the AFBF had an organization separate from that of the men, and Ruth Sayre began to preach the gospel of full partnership. She said, ''The advantages of partnership lie in the fact that women are creators of public opinion. As part of the Farm Bureau, they can more effectively cooperate in the Farm Bureau program. They can strengthen its membership and influence. They are important in building an attitude conducive to the understanding of farm problems.''

In October 1944, Ruth Sayre participated in a White House Conference on Rural Education, speaking on the panel that summarized the two-day session. She was well-informed on the topic, ''Building Rural Schools and Communities to Cope with the Problems of Tomorrow,'' which offset her diffidence at speaking to an audience of prominent educators in the White House East Room.

President Roosevelt addressed the group, saying, ''There are many things which we have learned in this war through the Selective Service system. We have found that among those examined, four-and-a-half percent can be classed as illiterate, and forty percent of all registrants have not gone beyond an elementary school education.''

Just as Ruth Sayre was reflecting that young men from the farms must have contributed heavily to those dismal statistics, the president said, ''The American form of government was conceived and created by men, most of whom had been taught in country schools.'' Country schooling had a noble history, and it could rise to meet the nation's needs again, Mrs. Sayre decided. She was more than ready to accept Roosevelt's challenge, ''We must lay plans for the peacetime establishment of our educational system on a better basis than we have ever known before.''

Eleanor Roosevelt also attended the sessions. Ruth Sayre had great respect for the First Lady, Democrat though she was. The two women saw eye to eye on many matters, and later, when Mrs. Roosevelt spoke at

Added Farm Bureau responsibilities in 1944 made family time even more precious to Ruth, seen here with Raymond, Alice, and John.

the Des Moines Coliseum, Ruth Sayre made the introduction with the consummate understatement that proved her admiration, "You all know Mrs. Roosevelt. Here she is."

Along with preparations for Christmas in 1944, Mrs. Sayre worked on details for special projects of the Associated Women, including a Seeds for Britain drive and the assembling of parcels for overseas war victims.

The new year, 1945, began with a round of speaking engagements at farm institutes, annual meetings, and county achievement days. Raymond said dryly, "Ruth can leave home at 9 o'clock in the morning and be anywhere in the state by noon."

She denied such superhuman speed, but she did spend a great deal of time in the car, and she wished she could discover a fabric that would allow her to arrive at her destinations unwrinkled.

Raymond was traveling frequently too, particularly to Omaha for Federal Land Bank board meetings. A Warren County newspaper editor noted that the Sayres met for breakfast in an Omaha hotel before going their separate ways.

Ruth Sayre's speaking circuit included agricultural colleges from Michigan to Mississippi, where she would talk to Farm and Home audiences. She challenged farm women to widen their horizons, to be "armed to the brain rather than to the teeth," and not to be bounded on the north by "What shall we have to eat?" on the south by "What shall I wear?" on the west by "the children" and on the east by "what John says."

She was concerned with changing the image of the farm wife as a worn-out drudge who relied on brawn rather than brains. During a planning session for the Farm Bureau's Annual Sports Festival, someone suggested a rolling pin contest for women, and Ruth Sayre disposed of it as deftly as she had demolished the beauty queen contest idea each time it was proposed. The committee agreed that her view of the farm wife as an active, intelligent, and attractive woman was more appealing than the image of a rolling pin–wielding termagant that such a contest would encourage.

The surface of the dining room table in the Ackworth farmhouse had not been seen for months. The paperwork involved in Ruth's many responsibilities kept it deeply covered with letters and reports. The dining room also accommodated a desk and files.

The massive effort of Iowa Farm Bureau women to improve rural education paid off in 1945, when the Fifty-second General Assembly passed a substantial number of bills presented by the School Code Commission. State aid to education was quadrupled at $13 million, county administration and county superintendent bills were passed, and important amendments were added to the reorganization and retirement laws. Transportation aid was renewed at $2 million, and the Agricultural Tax Credit was increased to $2 million with a ceiling of 15 mills on property tax on agricultural land.

The 1945 Iowa Farm Bureau convention was cancelled because of gas rationing, but the meeting of county delegates was held.

Mrs. Sayre was at home on the April day when Franklin Delano Roosevelt died in Warm Springs, Georgia. She said, "I got the news on the radio, and that was a sad day all around."

At that time she had not formed an opinion of Harry Truman, the new president, but he would appoint her to the Agricultural Research Policy Committee of the United States Department of Agriculture and to the United States Commission for UNESCO, and she later said, "I visited with him several times in his office. I thought he was more down-to-earth and more political than Hoover. I liked him, and I enjoyed our visits together."

Ruth Sayre planted a huge victory garden, and by the time she was harvesting tomatoes by the bushel, the A-bomb was dropped on Hiroshima and Nagasaki. The war was over, but the human destruction that signaled its end was sickening.

Bill would be coming home, and Helen was to be married August 18 to George Coolidge, whom she had met in Washington, and would start teaching in the public schools of Ashland, Massachusetts, at the beginning of the fall term. Alice was well situated in her government work, John was growing up bright and healthy on the farm, and Ruth Sayre realized how much she had to be thankful for in the newly peaceful world.

The season turned, and it was November. In the minute of silence on November 11, Ruth remembered that moment twenty-seven years earlier at Fort Worden on Puget Sound when she had thought, "It's over, and we've come through. Thank God!"

Eight days after Armistice Day, 1945, William Buxton, Jr., died of a cerebral hemorrhage while Ruth was attending a state Farm Bureau meeting in Des Moines. The whole town mourned with the family, and notice was given that all stores, banks, the City Hall, and the Warren County Courthouse would be closed at the hour of the funeral on Wednesday afternoon.

Ruth's sister Martha and her husband, John Scott, an Evanston executive, brought their family to Indianola for the funeral, and Bill Buxton and his wife Betty hurried home from Florida. Anna Buxton was strong in her grief, seeing to the comfort of her gathered family with her usual graciousness.

As the organ played in the Methodist church, Ruth remembered the strength of her father's arms when he carried her home from the pear tree, the expression on his face when she walked into the bank in her mother's long skirt, and his rich laugh when he unwrapped the glass diamonds. Losing him seemed unendurable, but it must be borne. Her shoulder pressed Raymond's for comfort, and he took her hand.

Iowa Farm Bureau women had been cooperating with the State Department of Health in a study of available medical services for several years, and the 1946 passage of the Hill-Burton hospital bill for improving rural health services was cause for celebration.

The education issue continued to be important to Ruth Sayre, and at a state meeting of the Farm Bureau women, she spoke to Dr. Malcolm Price, president of Iowa State Teachers College, about the scarcity of elementary school teachers, asking, "What are you doing about it at ISTC?"

Price answered that the college had a training program, but the enrollment was meager. He turned to the assembled women and asked, "How many of you are encouraging your children to become teachers?" Only a few hands were raised, and he said, "That is the problem. We won't have teachers for farm children until farm families encourage their youth to enter the teaching profession."

Ruth Sayre responded to the challenge with a proposal that the

In 1944 Ruth's parents took pride in her increasing prominence.

Iowa Farm Bureau women adopt a scholarship program to help rural young people attend college. The project was approved late in 1946.

At a summer meeting of the County Women's Council of the USA in Omaha in 1946, Ruth Sayre met Laura Lane, a reporter for *Country Gentlewoman* and a life member and ardent supporter of the Associated Country Women of the World.

Miss Lane says, "Mrs. Sayre always thought the Country Women's Council was poorly named. Originally, it was the United States Liaison Committee for ACWW, which she thought the group actually was, and she fought the changing of the name."

Laura Lane took an instant liking to Ruth Sayre, and she says, "The only weakness I ever observed in her was a human one—the reluctance to control her weight. She loved good food and was a good cook in the traditional Iowa sense. She was invited to many banquets and dinners, and like all of us, she found it hard to deprive herself. So, in my recollection, she was never willowy, but she never looked gross, either. Perhaps she would have if I had disliked her." (Laura Lane *was* willowy, a handsome career woman in her prime, when the two first met.)

Plans for the first postwar Triennial of the Associated Country Women of the World in Amsterdam were progressing, and the country women of the Netherlands were saving their ration stamps to feed their guests.

Ruth Sayre said, "In these times, the world is turning a corner and starting out on a new road. I wouldn't have missed the chance to help lay out the road and to be part of its building. Life today is like getting up on Monday morning to tackle the job of housecleaning. The place is a mess, a lot of hard work lies ahead, but what a lot of satisfaction to be at work again, cleaning up, building, and recreating! We women like order. We like cleanliness. Right now we want to begin to sweep up, to get things straightened out, clean and shining and orderly, so we can go about the business of raising our children in a decent world."

Her words expressed the feelings of countless rural women, and Laura Lane says, "The written speeches do not convey the electric atmosphere that surrounded much of what she was saying. I do not know of any woman speaker who could move an audience as significantly as she could. She made you want to commit yourself and be your best self, and she did this without using any of the oratory or platform tricks of the evangelist.

"I think it is hard to recognize what she did to women's awareness of themselves. This was a subject never discussed in those days. She never seemed daring herself in what she said, but she inspired others to dare—to think for themselves, to be themselves."

Ruth Sayre herself said, "People want to be challenged to do something big," and she offered such a challenge in her four-point statement of human rights: "1. Treat everyone with respect as you would your brothers and sisters. 2. Human rights have nothing to do with your bank account, religion, or color. 3. Everyone has the right to be alive. 4. Everyone should have the right to seek refuge from persecution in their own country by going to another."

In the hopeful summer of 1946 farmers were fairly well off. Prices for their products had risen through the war years, the rural mood was optimistic, and the Sayres had enough money to relax on the south shore of Iowa's Clear Lake when the harvest was accomplished.

Ruth began to collect some of the beautiful things she loved, particularly Staffordshire. The colonial American scenes painted by English artists on the tableware reminded her of her own family links with the British Isles. She also loved the strawberry motif, collecting anything that resembled the sweet, red berry.

Ever since the first time she bought a hat without maternal guidance, the straw with a crown of flowers purchased from her first paycheck, she had been in love with hats. At last the long years of deprivation were over, and she began to collect them, setting aside a special closet for them in the Ackworth farmhouse. As the collection grew, she took pleasure in giving talks about her hats.

When hard times receded into memory, Ruth Sayre was presented with corsages when she spoke, and she said, "I always liked them, even though they could be a nuisance sometimes." Roses, the flowers of her wedding bouquet, were her favorites.

Flowers were everywhere when the Sayres' son Bill married Ruthann Hermanson on June 7, 1947. The newlyweds lived in a third-floor attic apartment in Ames while Bill finished his senior year at Iowa State College, but, Mrs. Sayre said, "They were coming back to the farm, so we fixed up a hired man's house west and north of ours to have things ready for them."

By 1947 Ruth Sayre and Gertrude Dieken, woman's editor of the *Farm Journal,* had an excellent working relationship, which gave Mrs. Sayre another means of reaching farm women with her thoughts and ideas. Her by-line would appear in *Successful Farming, Women's Press,* and the *Home Economics Journal,* but she contributed most frequently to the *Farm Journal.*

In a 1947 issue of the *Farm Journal* she wrote, "You may argue that women do not like to study. They would rather do things with their hands. How are we to make the farm home a great stabilizing force in America? Not just with our hands, I believe, but mostly with our heads and hearts.

"Be leaders for Sunday School and church, 4-H, Home Demonstration Club, PTA, farm organizations, school affairs, and health projects. Do more than serve refreshments at school board meetings. Women must serve on the school board and other policy boards for the sake of our own homes. It is the duty of women to do for the community what they do for their own homes—keep it clean, orderly, and healthy—see that it has good education and is well governed. Guard its ideals. You don't have time? Stop talking on the phone so much, crocheting, and making quilts, and you'll find time for community homemaking."

One of Ruth Sayre's constant themes was the conflict between the Martha mind and the Mary mind. Laura Lane recalls that she described the Martha mind as bounded by the ironing board and the sink, referring to the biblical sister who fussed in the kitchen while Mary talked with Christ.

Miss Lane says, "I believe that no one ever thought of Mrs. Sayre as a feminist. She was always supremely feminine. We could, however, describe her as one of the early consciousness raisers because I believe that in the period between the end of World War II and her retirement from public life, she did more than any other person to liberate women from a false sense of inferiority."

Louise Rosenfeld notes, "She had power that got into one's soul. When I came in as state leader of Home Economics Extension, she made me think I could do things that I never thought could be done."

Ruth Sayre understood the thrust of the women's movement, and she said she was concerned for both men and women. "I wanted to improve the life of country people. The more I saw of it, the more sure I became that farmers were on the bottom rung of the ladder, and that was where everybody expected them to stay. That was what they expected themselves—work hard, make what you can, and enjoy country life."

Alice Van Wert Murray, who has in many ways followed in Ruth Sayre's footsteps (Farm Bureau, ACWW, Safety Council, and Iowa Mother of the Year), speaks of "the tremendous leadership Mrs. Sayre gave toward improving the life of farm women both at home and abroad—fired by both her genuine love for farm life and her firm belief in the blessings it bestowed beyond the advantages of city life at the time."

Ruth Sayre's opportunity for the expansion of her efforts was imminent.

10

A Global Concern

IN Amsterdam ACWW delegates met for the fifth Triennial at the Hague. Ruth Sayre said, "By 1947 we were living in a different and vastly changed world. Technology was turning farming from a way of life to a business. The women were ready to make the necessary changes, but Mrs. Watt had made an association too large and diverse to be held in shape by an informal constitution."

Even the English-speaking delegates did not speak the same language, they discovered, and the Americans did not understand the rules of procedure under which the ACWW operated.

"The English call the presiding officer the convenor, and the meeting arises, not adjourns," Mrs. Sayre said. She also noted that expressions of approval varied, the English saying, "Hear, hear!" the Scottish women stamping their feet, and the German woman pounding the table. "Luckily I had a chance to notice this before my talk began," she said, "or I wouldn't have known what to make of it."

She told the delegates, "It's time for farm women to learn the economic facts of life and discuss international affairs like we do the art of making slipcovers."

They knew she was one of them when she said, "One thing that makes country women feel so much at home with each other, I think, is that they have a common body of knowledge of the land and its life, and certainly we all have the problem of the weather in common!"

Ruth Sayre spoke to their condition, and, she said, "Farm women are pretty realistic. They have no time for anything that doesn't tie into their lives."

*Ruth Buxton Sayre, the working president of
ACWW, wrote letters by the score in 1947.*

In Amsterdam Ruth Sayre met Stella Bell, then "a youngish contributing member," who would become general secretary of ACWW in
1949 and whom Mrs. Sayre would regard as her "ACWW daughter."

Mrs. Bell says, "We were all keen to know who was going to be the
new world president, and I heard many delegates say that there was a
very good, capable American standing, but until she made her first
speech as the new president, this quiet American had not been very ob-
vious during the sessions. She made a wonderful speech, and it was ob-
vious that here was a leader."

Ruth Sayre said, "Several English women were eager to take over, but I feel that Mrs. Watt gave me the unofficial nod, realizing the importance of American support and dollars to rebuild the association. She had heard me speak at some of our state meetings and in Canada. Mrs. Watt knew exactly what she wanted to do and how she wanted it done. She made it very clear that it was *her* conference until the Triennial ended, and after the meeting in Amsterdam, she never came to another. She completely disappeared."

Until Mrs. Sayre took the position, the ACWW presidency was viewed as a title, an honor, a nominal office. It was not a decision-making job.

"I had different ideas," she said, "I planned to be a working president. I believed that women in other countries besides England must be involved in making policies to make the organization more representative of its membership."

The working presidency would be expensive, but, as Louise Rosenfeld puts it, "Mrs. Sayre had the know-how necessary to get money and tie leadership together." The American Farm Bureau Federation would pay her way to England, member organizations would finance her visits to their countries, the Canadian Institutes would be responsible for her expenses in Canada, and she would pay her own travel costs in the United States.

Until 1947 ACWW dues were voluntary, and the membership had not grown much from the twenty-two countries represented in 1933. Ruth Sayre put the delegates on notice that things would be different in the future, saying, "We have taken a tuck in time. We have put a pleat in space. We have let out the seams of our thinking."

The theme of her acceptance speech was "Unity is the outgrowth of diversity," and this idea would not be easy to sell at home.

Laura Lane says, "The Midwest between the two world wars was the most isolated part of the country, and this probably was due in part to the influence of the *Chicago Tribune,* whose management expressed almost daily contempt for royalty, abhorrence for Communism, and carried on a constant tirade against 'foreign involvement.' I believe that Mrs. Sayre, more than any other person, changed the public outlook from one of complete isolation to something closer to an international outlook."

In this effort, Ruth Sayre had the support of Allan Kline, who visited England and Europe several times after the end of the war and was the Farm Bureau's best-informed person on European relationships and needs.

The ACWW membership would offer some resistance to the ideas of the new president. Theoretically, the organization was democratic, but this was not so in practice. The executive committee was largely from England, and the other member groups named proxies who lived near London to vote for them. This was not Mrs. Sayre's idea of democracy.

When the Triennial ended, Ruth Sayre traveled on through Holland, Belgium, Switzerland, and England. The September sun starkly revealed the ruined heart of Rotterdam, devastated by Nazi bombs. Standing at the scene where, her guide said, 30,000 people lost their lives in less than eight minutes, she murmured, "They were people like you and me. It's one thing to read about this, but it is something else to see it with your own eyes!" The destruction chilled and numbed her, but certainly not to the point of inaction. Reconstruction must be tackled with all speed and with every resource.

The Netherlands and Belgium had suffered crop failures in the 1947 growing season, and in France she found a severe shortage of fertilizer, machinery, supplies, and labor. Everywhere Ruth Sayre went, she could see there were too many people to feed with the existing farm products. In the cities, food distribution was next to impossible, and the black market flourished.

She remembered the words of junketing congressmen who said they had seen no hungry people in Europe, and later she would tell them, "We talk about whether food is good or bad. They talk about whether there is enough food to keep body and soul together. Not enough food makes people irritable—low nutrition equals a low outlook on life!"

Ruth Sayre guessed that the problem of supplying food for Europe would continue for at least a decade. The outlook was bleak, and yet the forging of human bonds seemed promising. She said, "I could close my eyes in any farmhouse and by the conversation imagine I was back in Iowa."

Seeing so much desperate need, Mrs. Sayre was convinced that agricultural goods should be traded freely, and she expressed that view by saying, "If goods don't cross borders, soldiers will." Alice Murray notes that the comment has been borrowed widely without proper credit.

To those who congratulated her on her newest honor when she got home, Ruth Sayre said simply, "I was elected as an American, not as myself."

She told what she had seen in Europe, and her concern was not only for the war victims in the Allied countries, but for the vanquished as well. "I didn't see as much as I wanted to," she said, "I wasn't able to get a visa to go to Germany."

At the 1947 American Farm Bureau Federation convention, Ruth

Sayre appeared on the program for the first time. The keynote speaker was James Turner, president of the International Federation of Agricultural Producers, and the occasion was crucial to the Farm Bureau's commitment to international affairs.

Mrs. Sayre described the scarcity, want, and destruction she had seen in Europe a few months earlier and urged the acceptance of the Economic Recovery Program, the Marshall Plan to help Europe, and the Reciprocal Trade Agreements Act. She said, "We are in the front line of foreign policy because no problem is so fundamental as that of food. We must work for expanding trade."

Traditionally, farm people had wanted to keep foreign goods out, thinking this served their best interests, but Ruth Sayre adamantly repeated her deeply held belief, "If goods and services do not cross boundaries, sooner or later, soldiers will." She went on to say, "We are part of the world. We cannot resign from it." Her words carried weight, and the Farm Bureau did endorse the Trade Agreements Act.

Already gratified by the effect of her speech on the delegates, Mrs. Sayre took overwhelming pleasure in the election of her close friend and associate, Allan Kline, to the presidency of the AFBF. As Kline accepted the office, she recalled his narration of the pageant on the history of agriculture she had written for a state Farm Bureau event. She had stood behind the curtain and "punched him" when it was time for his lines, but Al Kline would need no prompting for this job, and he had the "international mind."

Ruth Sayre rushed home to prepare for Christmas, and the happiest news of that holiday season was Helen's announcement that she and George were expecting a baby. International greetings arrived at the Ackworth post office, including a photograph of Ruth drinking tea with ACWW delegates inscribed, "Remembering the happy days we spent in Amsterdam together."

Mrs. Sayre's involvement with the United Nations would grow in scope through the years, but the activity nearest her heart always would be the United Nations Education, Scientific and Cultural Organization (UNESCO). She became the AFBF representative to that body in 1948.

She would serve on the board of the UN Food and Agriculture Organization and on the Economic and Social Council, and she would steer the ACWW to the status of a nongovernmental organization within the UN, pressing for the Category A designation that allowed organizations to make recommendations to UN agencies.

In the spring of 1948 Ruth Sayre prepared for another trip to Europe. Before she left, her reflections on the 1947 trip appeared in the *Farm Journal* titled "Peace *is* Possible."

Describing her horrified response to the aftermath of the war, she wrote, "Utopian dreams of outlawing war overnight leave me cold. We cannot talk peace into existence. If we could, it would already be here. It boils down to this: If we would abolish war, we must learn to live and work with the people of the world as we learn to live and work with people of our own communities. This means finding peaceful ways to settle our differences—settling them by rules and laws which the world community sets up for itself.

"The root cause of war lies in our bitterness and hate, jealousies, ambitions, desire for revenge and power. The only answer to this is the conversion of the human heart to nobler purposes. Many causes of war are found in economic problems. As women, we haven't paid much attention to such problems. 'That is men's business,' we've said, and what we *meant* was that it was hard work, often dull work, to study economic information. We comfort ourselves by saying our place is in the home, then go outside the home to pick up the children, get the groceries, and deliver the cream. We forget that we are tied to the outside world by a thousand invisible strands.

"We can begin by studying about food. That is in our sphere. We can study the food needs of Europe—the way to meet these needs. We can understand the political effects of having people hungry. We can discuss the ways of opening doors to trade. We don't spend as much time in our club meetings studying world trade and European recovery programs as we do in discussing flower arrangements and the planning of our kitchens.

"Many of the decisions about economic problems that cause wars are not made in the UN, but in Congress. What we try to do in the United States has profound repercussions on the rest of the world. Can you influence the decisions of Congress? Yes! You can speak up for the things you believe in. Public opinion is one of the powerful forces that shapes the world. You may say, 'I am just one person.' True, but you *are* one. You make decisions every day. You vote (sometimes). You influence your husband. You affect the opinion of your neighbors. Look well to your opinion. It can count either for or against peace. You can influence Congress through people you elect to represent you there.

"Of course I am going to say you ought to vote. But I am going to be much more realistic than that. You must work through your own political party to get people to run for office. You must work in the caucus and the primary to nominate candidates whose political philosophy will support the measures you believe will build a peaceful world. If you don't do this, you may have no choice except between two unacceptable candidates."

Ruth Sayre once said, "It takes great strength to bring your life up square with what you think and keep it there." She was doing just that in the political arena of her home state.

Roger Fleming puts it this way: "I remember her role in helping to create the political climate that made it possible to nominate and elect a fellow Warren Countian, William Beardsley from New Virginia. The issues in the campaign were Farm Bureau women's issues—roads, schools, and taxes. All had suffered benign neglect in the administration of Governor Robert Blue, and Beardsley took advantage of the public's interest in action. Farm Bureau women throughout the state had played a major part in creating that interest under the leadership of Mrs. Sayre. She was the bridge to the male leadership, whose help and cooperation were indispensable."

William Beardsley defeated the incumbent in his own party in the Primary and went on to become governor of Iowa.

Packing for a journey that would include a meeting of the nongovernmental organizations of the UN in Geneva, the annual meeting of the ACWW in London, meetings with the Scottish Women's Institutes, and a trip to Germany if permission could be had, Ruth Sayre also packed two bags for 14-year-old John. He was going to summer camp while she was away and then on a trip to the West with his father.

Before she left, Mrs. Sayre learned that Roger Fleming, the coauthor of the "all we know in six easy lessons" pamphlets, was joining Allan Kline in the nation's capital as director of the American Farm Bureau Federation's Washington office. The Iowa brand of mutual respect between men and women in Farm Bureau work *certainly* should flourish now.

In Geneva, Switzerland, Mrs. Sayre spoke for farm women at a meeting of the UN Department of Public Information, then set off to meet Swiss farm women. She observed that the peasant women were part of a general farm organization called the Farmers' Union and that they worked fourteen to fifteen hours a day. She even broke down their activities into time slots: forty-four percent in the field or garden, twenty-five percent milking, nineteen percent cooking, and ten percent child care. With this kind of daily schedule, it was necessary for Swiss women's organizations to meet on Sunday.

She observed that the food situation was somewhat better than it had been in 1947, but food and feed still were below the prewar level, with most calories coming from bread and potatoes.

In England for the ACWW annual meeting, she noted, "The English have lower rations now than during the fighting. Many countries of Europe never have been self-sufficient in food, and the population has increased twenty-five percent. The farm labor situation is bad, fertilizer is lacking, and much of the livestock has been killed off.''

Ruth Sayre's clearance to visit Germany was delayed, but it finally went through. Then another problem arose. The plane was a military craft, and regulations required all passengers to wear pants to facilitate attaching a parachute to the body. Mrs. Sayre had no slacks, and postwar scarcity made it impossible for her to buy a pair. After long consultation, she was given permission to fasten the parachute to her back, becoming the only skirted person ever to fly in an army plane between Stuttgart and Berlin. During the flight she comforted and encouraged frightened and airsick young army wives.

She found Germany in a shambles. No building was whole, and the morale of the people was in the same shattered condition. Hitler had destroyed the German women's organizations, and Mrs. Sayre was convinced of the need to revive and rebuild them. Women outnumbered men in Germany, accounting for two-thirds of the voters. They also formed the backbone of the agricultural work force so badly needed to feed the nation.

Mrs. Sayre observed, ''German peasant women are almost beasts of burden! In the past, they were confined to church, children, and cooking. Women between the ages of fifteen and twenty-five have no sense of war guilt. They are quiet and skeptical of dogmas, and they have no ties to home and family. Most of them are morally and spiritually uprooted, knowing nothing but insecurity and distrust.

''Women between twenty-five and fifty are defensive and torn by war guilt. They are bitter, desolate, and sometimes unbalanced. Many are unable to think their own thoughts constructively. They feel insecure. Only the women over fifty have some feeling of security. They have a background of culture and a philosophy of life.''

In Berlin Mrs. Sayre was the guest of Louise Schroeder, mayor of the city. She said, ''I watched Louise Schroeder stand up to the Russians by refusing their currency, putting Berlin in the Allied camp.''

Talking with Americans in Berlin, Mrs. Sayre discovered that they considered the Russians to be basically weak and expected a long stretch of cold war conditions. She also observed that American life in Berlin was placid and isolated from the Germans.

At the end of her stay in Germany, she formulated what she would say to the people at home: ''We must not be disillusioned if we find that the Marshall Plan is not enough to solve Europe's economic problems. It is not a relief program, it is a recovery program. The women in Germany know what war means. We must forgive them and help them work for democracy and the establishment of a new government.''

Knowing that she must return to Germany as soon as possible,

Ruth Sayre went home to share what she had learned in the land of the former enemy.

"They wanted me to visit more countries in Europe," she said, "but I wanted to be with Helen when the baby came."

The birth of George Ruggles Coolidge, III, on July 18, 1948, in Framingham, Massachusetts, made Ruth Buxton Sayre a grandmother for the first time, and she was enthralled with "Ruggie."

Following that happy interlude, she demonstrated what United Press radio described as "keen, intelligent eyes that flash fire when she talks about the misfortunes of the world." She said, "People are downright hungry—hopelessly so. It's impossible to be optimistic about anything when you think about food in the daytime and dream about it at night. Sending food to Europe is our chance to help save Western Europe for Democracy. The people there are not starving, just hungry with a hunger that hasn't been satisfied in years."

At Ackworth, the August 1948 issue of *Holiday* magazine was waiting on the dining room table. Its spread on "The Corn Belt" featured Ruth Buxton Sayre as one of Iowa's leaders in the company of Henry Wallace; Ruth Suckow, novelist; Virgil Hancher, president of the State University of Iowa; George Gallup, the pollster; B. J. Palmer, head of the Palmer College of Chiropractic in Davenport; and Donna Reed, the film star from Denison.

11

Another Gavel

FOR years people had been marveling at how much Ruth Sayre could accomplish. She managed it by careful planning, and in a tiny, undated notebook from her Farm Bureau state chairman days, the penciled notations for a stretch of April read like a litany of Iowa counties: Poweshiek, Buena Vista, Keokuk, Warren, Wapello, Page, Buchanan, Union—one a day—then two days in Indianapolis and back to Des Moines and Ames, Iowa.

By 1948 she was even busier. Requests for speeches were constant, and unless she had a conflicting engagement, she was ready to oblige. She covered sheets of hotel stationery from every part of the United States with notes for speeches.

She worked tirelessly for UNESCO and the Rural Welfare Committee of the UN's Food and Agriculture Organization, served as a trustee for the National Society for Crippled Children and Adults, attacked the presidential duties of ACWW with zeal, and participated fully in the affairs of the Associated Women of the American Farm Bureau Federation.

She said, "I have always considered myself as a mouthpiece for other rural women. What I wanted to say was important to me, and I thought it probably was what other farm wives would say if they had a chance."

Few of them did have the chance to travel, observe, and form educated opinions that Ruth Sayre had. For instance, when she spoke at the National Home Demonstration Council Convention banquet in Tulsa, Oklahoma, in early October 1948, her topic was "Europe Revisited," and she said, "The smaller the world, the more tolerance and Christian grace it is going to take to live in it. We have got to learn to live in the world peacefully, creatively, with all the differences. We all want the same things, but we don't all want to get them the same way.

"We must face the fact that there are many basic differences between countries, between peoples, between organizations. We cannot make everyone over in the same pattern. We should not if we could. Let me repeat what I said to you last year: the smaller the world becomes in size—the nearer we live together—the more difficult the problem of human relationships becomes. One of the ways this can be met is to encourage the visits of farm women leaders in our country . . . I am convinced that wherever you go in the world, you will find farm women carrying on the same kind of meetings."

Ruth Sayre would have to agree that the male members of farm families in other countries might not be as obliging as her own husband and sons.

Raymond and John were well trained in taking care of themselves when the wife and mother of the household was away. Raymond did the cooking, and when the meal was over, John shooed him out of the kitchen and accomplished the cleanup. In earlier years Ruth had tried to prepare food in advance and leave it for her men, but, she says, "Raymond always cooked something else, and my food would still be there when I got back." Apparently her family never felt abandoned, just proud of their ability to fend for themselves and proud of her and the well-deserved praise she received.

Honors and offices did not change Ruth Buxton Sayre. Louise Rosenfeld, who went from Extension to the Iowa State College faculty, called Mrs. Sayre "a homey kind of person," saying, "She can talk about how her roses are doing as well as about affairs of state and is just as interested in one as in the other. Once after what was considered a very important state meeting, she said, 'I'm going home to work in the garden, and there I can accomplish something!' She stayed a real farm woman."

Huge audiences never deflected Ruth Sayre from what Alice Murray calls "the homespun touch of true-to-life happenings delivered with her contagious chuckle. She was a popular speaker with both men and women, and her speeches were used as good examples. For instance, when she spoke at the National Farm Institute in Des Moines, a Drake University speech instructor brought his classes to listen to her. Her organization of thought and delivery were superb, and her messages had depth."

On a one-to-one basis, Ruth Sayre was a delightful companion, according to Laura Lane, who says, "I remember a small mining town in

West Virginia where we sat up most of the night talking to pass the time. She had a great sense of humor which came to her rescue, and beyond that, she was good and pleasant company. The hours always seemed shorter and less tedious because of her conversation.''

Ruth Sayre also had conversations with herself as a means of measuring her commitment and taking stock of her capabilities. Her election to the presidency of the Associated Women of the American Farm Bureau Federation was inevitable, and early on the day when this would happen at the 1948 annual meeting of the Associated Women in Atlantic City, she moved briskly along the boardwalk, considering how she would handle another important responsibility.

The American Farm Bureau Federation was the largest farm organization in the nation and in the world. The presidency of the Associated Women would give her a seat on the AFBF board and a vote in its policymaking. The job would be demanding—even overwhelming—but with two good Iowa friends in top positions, Allan B. Kline as president and Roger Fleming as secretary-treasurer, she believed that she could manage it. They would be working together as they had in Iowa a decade before.

And they had their work cut out for them. Postwar surpluses and inflation were troubling farmers. Prices for farm products were taking a dive after a steady climb through the war years, and farmers were receiving ninety cents an hour for their labor. The Farm Bureau, more concerned about freedom than about security, believed that a free economy could produce a fair relationship between farm and nonfarm prices.

The question within the Farm Bureau was how this fair relationship could be reached. Some members wanted flexible price supports and others argued for rigid price supports at ninety percent of parity. Debate was heated.

Roger Fleming says, "I remember Mrs. Sayre's mental toughness on the AFBF board of directors. As the only woman, she might have asked for—and received—special consideration. She did not. Instead, she worked at being a responsible board member. The more controversial the issue, the more difficult the decison, the better she functioned. This created respect on the part of the male board members and provided the essential basis for an effective relationship on the board. It also provided an example for Farm Bureau women.''

Parity, a word that was tossed about with incomplete understanding by many, was well understood by Ruth Sayre. It represented the equality of purchasing power for farmers with the other segments of society—a fair ratio between the prices of things farmers sold and the prices of what they bought, using a base period of known prosperity as the standard—1910–1914, the climax of the so-called golden years of

American agriculture. Ruth Sayre wryly noted that she did not come to farming until the gold had disappeared. Saturday's child, she had indeed worked hard for a living.

With her usual calm good sense, Mrs. Sayre tried to still the qualms of those who feared that parity for farmers would ruin the national economy. She said, "Farm prices under the parity formula would not increase unless other costs in the economy—wages and industrial prices—were also rising. Parity is not a fixed price, but it is a relationship formula."

The Farm Bureau opposed the Brannan Plan, which involved compensatory payments and cheaper food for the consumer at the expense of the producer. When the Brannan Family Farm Policy Review attempted to make government agencies the spokesmen for farmers, Ruth Sayre remembered the same battle in Iowa years before and joined the fray to preserve the right of farmers to speak for themselves.

Her energetic activity for the AFBF was noted particularly by Roger Fleming, who says, "She caused me to better understand and appreciate the contribution a fine woman leader can make to the successful functioning of an organization like the Farm Bureau."

As Ruth Sayre earned her own equality in the Farm Bureau, she pressed to extend it to the entire membership of the Associated Women. She said, "A membership of both men and women makes a more balanced approach to matters. After all, problems have no gender, so let us have the ideas of both sexes. One of the greatest obstacles to the progress of women is their acceptance of so many things as inevitable."

Carrie Chapman Catt, who had been president of the National Woman Suffrage Association during Ruth Buxton Sayre's college years, died in 1948, but many of her ideas lived on in the president of the Associated Country Women of the World and the Associated Women of the American Farm Bureau Federation. "Organize! Organize! Organize!" said Carrie Chapman Catt, and Ruth Sayre did. "Expose youselves to the other side" was another piece of advice from the great suffragette that Mrs. Sayre took seriously. "What is knowledge without action?" asked Carrie, and this was Ruth's question too.

The double presidential duties that made Mrs. Sayre the leader of millions of farm women all over the world caught the attention of the press, and Laura Lane says, "She had to spend a great deal of time with reporters individually. In spite of this, she never seemed to lose her good humor, and she paid the press the tribute of realizing that the reporters had some responsibility to the facts and to their readers and that they deserved wooing, not with any personal favors but with real insight into issues that often were complex. Mrs. Sayre had one quality you seldom see in leaders—alas, I must say—in women leaders of the past. She was never petty and could separate personalities from issues.''

Besides a penetrating analysis of issues, Ruth Sayre also gave reporters a part of herself. In a 1949 interview she said, ''The main objective of all these organizations I belong to is to better the life of farm women all over the world. Of course, I do lose touch with my old friends—that is one of the prices one pays for traveling so much.'' She went on to say how much she enjoyed feeding the chickens and that she allowed two days a week for heavy housework like washing, ironing, and cleaning and ''a couple of days of desk work. I couldn't operate without a schedule.''

In the spring of 1949 that schedule included what was for her the all-important return to Germany. The Cultural and Educational Relations Division of the United States Army engaged her to act as a visiting expert consultant. She was to teach German women how to form and conduct organizations in a democratic manner and was asked to make recommendations to the military government for Germany.

The German she had learned from Blanche Smith in high school and from Hildegarde Jend at Simpson needed brushing up, and before the trip, Mrs. Sayre practiced the language for hours with a German refugee in Des Moines.

Her German headquarters was a Frankfurt hotel, and she traveled in the American, British, and French zones, inspecting farms, kitchens, cellars, and barns. Many of the homes she visited were crowded with extra families who had fled the Russian sector.

She wrote home, ''What do you say to the German woman with whom you once fought—wanted to destroy? I hardly knew what to say. One woman took both my hands with tears in her eyes and said, 'I am so glad you have come. You are the first who has come to us, and we have long been separated from the world. Forgive us and help us.' She was not a German, she was a human being.''

In another letter she described how hard the German women worked and wrote, ''I'm glad I'm not a German woman!''

Believing that the education of German children was the key to the future, Ruth Sayre visited many schools with the traditional curriculum: agriculture for boys and home economics for girls. She confessed that after touring ''every inch of two schools and several farms, my feet were killing me!''

The kitchen in the Ackworth farmhouse was being remodeled in her absence according to the planning she had done with the Extension Service, and she made more long-distance suggestions, closing with a reminder to John, ''Don't forget to wash your hair.''

In 1949 Ruth Sayre weighed 180 pounds, and she was embarrassed to appear so well-fed from the bread basket of the world in the midst of Germans still showing the effects of wartime malnutrition. In one German orphanage her heart went out to the poor undersized children who, she assumed, had not eaten their fill for years. Later, in a casual conversation with a German official, she learned that "this was the normal size for people of that section, who are not naturally large like the Prussians we commonly picture as typical Germans."

The plight of German women disturbed Ruth Sayre. They could not afford laborsaving devices, and she reflected, "Extension Service information based on household research could frequently help the German housewife make her work easier without the expenditure of money."

She was pleased to find a love of beauty in the homes of Bavarian women and said, "This is something we could copy. They are willing to take time and trouble to make a small farmhouse attractive." Along with her compliments, she gave them vegetable seeds donated by Iowa 4-H clubs.

Arranging for the visit of several German women to the United States, Mrs. Sayre also recommended an educational program for German women to help them develop into active, responsible citizens of the community. She worked with the office of the military government of Bavaria for three weeks and noted, "The people of the German communities need to get together to discuss their needs and decide on projects on which they feel they could use scientific information. They may want to know about higher egg production or how to get more milk."

She admired the centuries-old Bavarian tradition of dating farms above the doors, but she said, "The farmer is tied to the agricultural procedures of his father and grandfather. He should attempt to keep all the old that is good, yet change his practices to fit into modern agriculture and industry."

The farms were too small for efficiency, Mrs. Sayre observed. German farming was more like gardening, and it required a great deal of labor, mostly performed by women.

She wrote, "The crux of the question for us in America will be our decision to 'keep on' until the job is done. That means, I think, that we must persist in appropriating funds to Europe longer than we had at first expected. We must keep open the channels of trade—through such devices as the Reciprocal Trade Agreement—we must support such measures as the International Wheat Agreement. We must stay on the job long enough to accomplish what is necessary in Germany. The Germans are not ready to govern themselves. Many Germans are afraid to cooperate with us for fear we will pull out and leave them at the mercy of the Communists. There will need to be a long, patient American occupation of Germany if we want democracy over there to be more than an ivory tower democracy. This is a job we have never attempted before.

"Since the war, life is hard in Germany. The monumental destruction of German cities gives you a dead feeling in the pit of your stomach. We must turn our energies toward the solution of the greatest human problem that faces the world—the plight of the world's children—the millions who are homeless and orphaned; who are without faith and hope and love. They lack love, care, and guidance. We cannot build a good world without getting at the children."

In Velpke, Mrs. Sayre met Lucie Boeck, one of the German women who would visit the United States with funds raised by American Farm Bureau women. The other was Marie Bauer. Frau Boeck would see a better way of life and return home with new yearnings. After her American visit, she wrote, "In Germany we have no automatic washing machine. That is still my dream of wishing. But so long I have to wash with my hands. The work in a farm never is to end and there are only the months January and February when we have any rest to ourselves. The children become elder so quick and then they must go to boarding school. My husband and I are alone again. That is the fate of all countrymen in Germany, where we have not such a nice school bus as you have in America."

Ruth Sayre remembered the days when there was no "nice school bus" for her own children and the hard struggle to achieve that convenience. She could identify with Lucie Boeck, having lived with hardship until she could do something about it, and she could tell her German friend with complete confidence that there would be better days.

An ambassador without portfolio for two months, Ruth Sayre looked, listened, and remembered. In her wide reading she had encountered the writings of Tagore, and these words of his became even more meaningful to her: "Thou hast made me know the friends that I knew not. Thou hast given me seats in homes not mine own. Thou hast brought the distant near and made a brother of a stranger."

Saturated with what she had seen, heard, and experienced, Ruth Sayre knew that it was time to go home. At Ackworth, Raymond and John hugely enjoyed her delight in the new kitchen. A door had been moved to fit the refrigerator into a U-shaped plan, excessive hardware on the cabinets had been removed, and the counter elevations were adjusted to her five-foot-five height. Counter tops and cupboard linings were strawberry red, picking up the shade of the latticed strawberries in the ceiling wallpaper, and John had painted the handles of all her old wooden spoons a matching red. And there were still more surprises.

Ruth Sayre
returned from
Germany in 1949
to the joys of
a remodeled
kitchen in
the Ackworth
farmhouse.

Baby lambs were
one of the delights
of country living
for the Sayres in
1948.

Raymond was busy with Farm Credit and Iowa Purebred Sheep Breeders Association, but he had found time to create an ornamental fish pool and a picnic fireplace in the yard with John's help, and they had plans for remodeling the sun porch.

Remembering the crowded European homes she had visited, Ruth Sayre took grateful pleasure in her own home. The living room, which extended the width of the house, was carpeted in dubonnet with walls of a serene, greenish gray. The pillars that once divided living room and dining room had been replaced by bookcases. Hooked rugs, family antiques, and corner shelves for precious pieces of china added to the homey look.

When the *Farm Journal* featured the Sayre home, Rachel Martens and Naomi Shank commented, "The charm, comfort, and taste you see pictured here are not the work of a decorator. They came from the thought and planning of a busy farm woman who realized that no matter how many other things need to be done, her family's happiness comes first."

Ruth Sayre said, "All along, ours has been a family project. Everybody pitched in, and now we all enjoy it."

The remainder of the year would be a rush of engagements, including a series of meetings in Canada, a Food and Agriculture Organization conference, a meeting of the International Federation of Agricultural Producers, and a speaking engagement in New Orleans. Mrs. Sayre's itinerary put her in Washington near Thanksgiving, and she decided to spend the holiday with her daughter Alice, whom she called "my most outspoken child—the one who said, 'I like Mother best of all.' "

That visit was all too short, so it was prolonged by Alice's decision to fly home with her mother. As they were winging toward Des Moines, Ruth Sayre remembered riding a coach car in the train during the war years and added planes to her reasons for giving thanks.

Searching for Raymond in the airport crowd as she always did at homecoming, Mrs. Sayre saw only Bill and John, and she could read the distress on their faces before they were close enough to speak.

Alice called to her brothers, asking the question Ruth Sayre was almost afraid to voice, "Where's Dad?"

"He cut his hand and went to the doctor." John said.

Then Bill pulled his mother aside and told her that the farmhouse had burned the day after Thanksgiving.

Her first reaction was one of deep relief that her family was intact— or almost so. She had yet to hear how Raymond had cut his hand. Then she thought of her beautiful new red and white kitchen—burned, ruined. It was hard to smile, but she managed it, saying, "Well, I guess we'll just have to put it back together again."

A wiring defect had caused the fire, which started in the basement and burned through the floors above. The damage was so extensive that the Sayres lived with Bill and Ruthann until June 1950, when the restoration was completed.

Learning of the fire, ACWW members held showers for Ruth Sayre to replace linens, rugs, and other household goods, and the house regained its former beauty. Before she left it after forty-six years, John took pictures of all the rooms to remember it just the way it was. By then he was a professional decorator, and he says, "The Ackworth home was large and well built—quite impressive with an abundance of trees and shrubs in the yard. I am sure that at the time of the fire in 1950 Mother and Dad could have built a new house with less effort and money than it took to rebuild the shell of our home. The possibility of building another home was, thankfully, never discussed."

12

Ideas with Hands and Feet

IN 1950 Ruth Sayre led the Farm Bureau women in their cooperation with the Rural Division of the American Medical Association. She spoke at many national and state health conferences on prepaid health insurance and other issues, and she continued her work on the U.S. Department of Agriculture's Council on Rural Health executive committee and on the Commission on Chronic Illness.

At the same time, the Farm Bureau women were deeply involved with the Farm Foundation's Committee on Rural Education and with the Rural Department of the National Education Association.

The first program planning committee of state leaders for the Farm Bureau women was appointed in 1950, giving new leaders an opportunity to serve. The continuing effort to work new leadership talent into the organization was an article of faith with Ruth Sayre. This new group was charged with evaluating and coordinating the women's program for the year, and its members produced a well thought-out plan.

This was a Triennial year for the Associated Country Women of the World, with the conference scheduled for September in Copenhagen. Stella Bell, longtime general secretary of the ACWW, has said, "If you work for ACWW, your whole life is geared to the Triennial." Ruth Sayre devoted a great deal of time to planning the Triennial, but her other responsibilities precluded gearing her whole life to it.

The theme of the meeting in Denmark was to be "Rural Welfare," and Mrs. Sayre invited Margaret Hockin, a Canadian member of the Food and Agriculture Organization's Rural Welfare Division, to address the delegates.

In May Ruth Buxton Sayre was named Iowa's Mother of the Year. This was the year when the American Mother's Committee, supported by the Golden Rule Foundation since 1933, was made a separate corporation "to develop and strengthen the moral and spiritual fiber of the American home," and the organization helped American Indians, needy schools, and children. Its aims were in complete accord with Mrs. Sayre's, and she knew, as much of the public did not, that a Mother of the Year was not expected to conform to a stay-at-home stereotype.

She said, "You have to make a lot of sacrifices when you do community service, and your family must sacrifice too. But there are compensations. Children respect a mother who is making a contribution to the community because she is a person in her own right. They become self-reliant adults. You must have a missionary feeling for community work. It helps withstand the criticism of those who do not approve of what you are doing."

Ruth Sayre was not the kind of person whom people would criticize openly, but she must have felt the tacit disapproval of those who lived their lives differently. In spite of this, she practiced what she preached, "Choose the place where you are needed most and concentrate on it."

Roger Fleming says, "I remember what a wonderful mother she was. I knew Helen, Alice, Bill, and John, and in addition to love for their parents, they had a deeply felt affection based on respect for a most worthwhile person."

The Sayres became grandparents twice in 1950. On August 4, Cynthia Ann was born to Helen and George Coolidge in Massachusetts, and there was sadness mixed with joy because Cindy's twin did not survive. Another grandchild, William Raymond, would be born to Bill and Ruthann Sayre on October 16, while Ruth Sayre and Alice were cruising on the Rhine after the Copenhagen Triennial.

Now another generation would inherit the good, solid values Ruth Sayre so often extolled in her speeches. She would say, "I have always believed that the farm home is the best place in the world to raise a family. There the child can be more easily trained in the habits that form good character. There family life is stable and sound. More emphasis must be put on homemaking and less on skills of housekeeping—whether you hang out a white wash or bring good food to a potluck."

Although Helen was a city dweller now, her outlook had been formed in a farm home. She had learned the "attitudes of reasonableness, generosity, and tolerance" that her mother talked about so often, and she never would forget the glad bonus of a day when the hay stacker broke down in the middle of the afternoon and

Daddy invited her to ride along to town to get the parts. Ruth Sayre need not worry about the upbringing of her city grandchildren.

She was, however, "distressed and unhappy at the plight of European children." She had seen for herself how the war had warped their values, making lying and cheating a way of life in occupied countries, and she was determined to help them find some of the normal happiness of childhood.

Anna Buxton, Ruth's mother, did not seem well in the summer of 1950, but the family did not consider this to be unusual because, Mrs. Sayre said, "She had peritonitis when she was young, and she never did get over the effects."

The illness worsened, and as the Copenhagen Triennial dates drew closer, Anna Buxton entered the Indianola hospital for surgery. Considering her mother's condition, Ruth Sayre was torn with anguish. She stood before the copy of the Cluny tapestry, "The Lady and the Unicorn," which Anna Buxton had given to a Simpson College dormitory, and tried to come to terms with the inevitable parting. Should she stay home to be with her mother? Could the ACWW do without a president at the Triennial? The lady in the tapestry had no answers, but Anna Buxton did.

"You must go, Ruth," she said from her hospital bed, "they need you." They held each other tenderly and said good-bye.

Packing with a heavy heart, Ruth reviewed all the ways Anna Buxton had helped her gain the position that now parted them: caring for the children, encouraging her to accept responsibility, praising her for her accomplishments. The irony of it brought tears to her eyes.

The American delegation to the Triennial headed by Mrs. W. E. Nichols of Lexington, Kentucky, numbered just over 200. Knowing that they would meet Danish royalty, the women practiced the curtsey aboard the *Queen Mary*. Ruth thought she was achieving the proper dignity in the unaccustomed bobbing gesture, and as she prepared to try once more, a steward brought her a cable.

Without looking at Raymond's message, she knew what it said. Mamma was gone. Anna Buxton had died of postsurgical pulmonary thrombosis. Numbly, Ruth Sayre made her way to the stern of the great liner and stared at its wake in the sea while she said a second farewell to her mother. Then she went to her cabin for a Bible and found an isolated deck chair where she could be alone to read her mother's favorite passages.

Later, Raymond would send her a copy of the eulogy in the First Methodist Episcopal Church of Indianola, where Anna McLaughlin Buxton had been president of the Woman's Home Mission and constant in the doing of good works for so many years. It spoke of her culture, urbanity, and grace. Ruth's private eulogy dwelt on love, faith, honesty, and high standards in every phase of life. Mamma!

In time Mrs. Sayre would learn of the terrible moment Alice suffered in Cyprus when her section chief came to her and said, "A wire has just arrived to the effect that your mother has died. We're terribly sorry!" Stunned, Alice asked to see the wire and learned that it was "Mamma," as she always called her grandmother. Sad as this news was, she had been expecting it, and she was overwhelmed with relief that "Mother" was still alive.

Anna Buxton had told Ruth not to waste time and strength in mourning, but to do her duty, and the time for that was near. In the years since Amsterdam, the ACWW had been occupied with postwar reclaiming and rebuilding. Now the organization must concern itself with growth and with becoming more representative of its membership.

Alice Murray says, "Mrs. Sayre inspired the structuring of working groups to involve the membership in exchanging ideas as a way of solving problems and developing leadership. She loved to see younger members develop their potential, and she insisted that memberships should be involved in policymaking. She observed that the structure of the organization must be changed so that more people from countries other than England, where the central office was located, should take an active part in business affairs. She was an advocate of democracy in action."

The business of the conference included adopting several changes in the constitution to bring the separate societies into closer touch with all phases of ACWW work. Mrs. Sayre considered the most important accomplishment to be the agreement to group societies in areas, each area to nominate its own vice-president, and the vice-presidents were not to be officers in name only. They were to be responsible for spreading information and encouraging new memberships in ACWW in their own areas.

Another change in the constitution was the revocation of voting power given contributing members in the annual meeting, which made it possible for direct representatives of societies to vote at a conference rather than express themselves through proxies. Ruth Sayre wanted the societies to have more voice in ACWW decisions.

In her first term, Mrs. Sayre had been a working president, and she was given the mandate to continue in this fashion by her reelection to the office in Copenhagen.

The one tense situation at the conference was the reaction to the German women's groups. Women of nations that had suffered terribly under Nazi conquest were unwilling to hear the greetings of their former enemies, and they made their feelings known.

"If we are going to rebuild," Ruth Sayre said, "the Germans must be members too."

Reluctantly, the dissenting delegations accepted her insistence and listened when she told them they must make possible "friendly person-to-person contacts beyond the scope of governments." A reporter at the sessions wrote, "By the end of the conference, the mere mention of Mrs. Sayre's name from the floor brought prolonged applause."

In her own good-natured and reasonable way, Ruth Sayre had made reconciliation possible, and the Landsfrauen-Verein of Germany became an affiliate of ACWW.

After all the practice on the *Queen Mary*, Ruth Sayre's curtsey to Danish royalty was performed under less than ideal circumstances. She met King Frederick, Queen Ingrid, the Danish princesses, and the Dowager Queen Alexandrine on the steps of Christianborg Castle, where a large meeting was to be held in the Parliament Rooms.

Mrs. Sayre was wearing her "hat for royalty," according to Stella Bell, who says, "We all loved the hat, and it became almost a friend. It's very human for a woman to feel her best in a smart hat."

At tea in the royal palace, fewer formalities were required, as the Danish monarchs were noted for their unpretentiousness, but Mrs. Sayre said, "I saw a fellow standing there, and I didn't know if he was the king or an equerry. I had to decide whether to bow. I did, and it was the king. The king and queen spoke English and talked to us about the women's organization and what they were doing."

Ruth Sayre also had tea with American Ambassador Eugenie Anderson, and they were photographed in animated conversation. Laura Lane remarks, "You could look at the picture and wonder which was the ambassador and which was the private citizen. Mrs. Sayre must have had a great source of inner strength, because she always seemed at ease in the presence of kings, queens, and prime ministers."

Danish hospitality was overwhelming, and Stella Bell recalls, "One evening a few of us were eating a late dinner in the little cafe next to the conference headquarters hotel when Mrs. Sayre, looking very travel worn, arrived, sank into a chair, and ordered a grilled steak— nothing else. She had been out all day visiting Danish members and had been entertained seven times. Seven times she had faced a table groaning with delicious, rich Danish pastries, and she said, "I knew I had to eat or my hostesses couldn't, and they were having one party each—but oh, I don't want to see anything sweet for a very long time!"

Reporting on the Copenhagen conference for *Country*

Ruth Sayre, wearing her "hat for royalty," met the Dowager Queen Alexandrine of Denmark on the steps of Christianborg Castle in 1950.

Gentlewoman, Laura Lane called it the most successful in the history of the organization. The women discussed technical assistance to less developed areas, and a Norwegian delegate said ruefully, "Water comes first to the stable, then to the kitchen." A Dutch woman said it might take many generations before everyone would like spinach.

Miss Lane observed the difference between Mrs. Sayre and her predecessor in the ACWW presidency, Mrs. Alfred Watt, saying, "Mrs. Watt once said to me, 'I am only eloquent when speaking of myself,' and that was true. She expected to be treated as the Queen Bee, and she was. Mrs. Sayre presented an entirely different kind of personality to the millions of women she dealt with. Mrs. Sayre often had opposition and battles, but she conducted them in a ladylike manner. She never made personal slurs or appeared to carry a grudge or seemed vindictive."

Ruth Sayre sent delegates from twenty-three countries home from this "wonderful meeting" in Copenhagen with these words, "We cannot go back altogether to yesterday's patterns, either in our organization or in the wider areas of our social and economic life. Many former patterns are as inadequate as last year's clothing for growing children. . . . Our organization must be international in character. It must reflect in deed and in truth the whole membership. May I say to you as you go home to the four corners of the world, go forth in faith and action—for you are going home to do the work that nobody else's hands can do." Of course she wanted them to work with their heads, too. Her motto was: "Give hands and feet to ideas."

In December Ruth Sayre addressed the annual convention of the Associated Women of the American Farm Bureau Federation in Dallas, beginning her speech with a nod to Professor Goodenough. She read Carl Sandburg's poem, *We, the People,* stressing the freedom stanza.

She spoke of the difficult international situation, saying, "Women are being called to account these days," and quoting Philip Wylie's "Mom is a jerk!" she identified the statement as a call to some soul searching.

"What kind of women do these years demand?" she asked. "On the whole, the farm homemaker has earned her right to prestige and respect in our democracy. She has labored to produce food and fiber with which to feed and clothe America; she has produced children to repopulate it. She has conscientiously cleaned her home and children with equal vigor. She has fed salads to her protesting husband and spinach to her protesting children. She has scrimped and saved and managed and at the same time tried to keep her nose powdered and her seams straight. Within her own bailiwick, the home, the farm woman has not fallen down on the job to any greater extent than other groups in our economy. On the other hand, I think we must admit that we do have much to learn about our role as citizens in a modern world."

She urged her audience to rethink "more clearly and precisely what we believe to be the aims and the duties of women in this kind of world." Listing the laudable aims of the Farm Bureau women, she said, "There is no evidence in them that we recognize our responsibility as world citizens." She told the Associated Women, as she had told the ACWW, "The former pattern that once seemed good for all time is as inadequate as last year's clothing for growing children."

Warning them against isolating themselves from the mainstream of economic and political life, she urged better information on public questions. But, she said, "Women shy away from keeping informed. We *say* we like to do things with our hands—make quilts, stir up a cake, play bridge. What we *mean* is that it's hard work, often dull work to study, digest information, and think out our own ideas clearly. It is apathy more than anything else that hampers us."

To challenge the women to make full use of their political rights, Ruth Sayre told the story of the Italian woman elected to office in 1945, the first year women had the vote in Italy. "Will women play a big part in Italian politics?" the woman was asked, and she said, "Yes! After twenty-two years of fascism, the war, the Nazi occupation, the clandestine struggle, and then the victory, Italian women know that politics is the health of their family, the food for their babies, the security of their homes, and the education of their children."

Having fought for peace for many years, Ruth Sayre was beginning to put it second on her list of priorities. What was more important? Freedom, and she saw it threatened by a burgeoning federal bureacracy and a general attitude of peace at any price.

At a Chicago Farm Bureau meeting, she said, "What is involved in this world crisis is that we now choose between two opposing courses of action. The one is freedom for the individual; the other is the subordination of the individual to the state. I am concerned that we do not become so absorbed with the goal of peace that we forget the goal of freedom. The age-old struggle for freedom is the fundamental issue of our time."

Together with her notes for this speech, she carried a note to herself, "Get blue shoes, oilcloth for shelves, boxes for Christmas things." Once again she would rush through preparations for the holiday, but it would be the first Christmas in her life that her mother would not share.

Among hundreds of Christmas greetings was one from Derby, England, which read, "I was listening to the radio, and the minister asked us to remember the things which brought us joy in 1950. My thoughts turned immediately to you. My mind was turned so often to the pleasure of the Copenhagen conference. How rich you are in all the things that matter!"

13

Self-confidence for Farm Women

AT home and abroad Ruth Sayre was the living example of an articulate woman who realized that world affairs were her affair. She did much to motivate other women to move in a similar direction, but it was a slow process.

"It has been the custom since Bible times to depend on women only to cook the dinner," she said, noting, "Farmers are always the most conservative—especially about women."

Even so, as Laura Lane observes, she made women "believe in themselves. For example, I never heard her talk about discrimination. I'm not sure she was aware of it, but she really declared war on that 'just a housewife' attitude, and she had some interesting ways of changing women's attitudes toward themselves—their image of themselves as second-class citizens. In many of her speeches she deplored the 'Martha mind' bounded by the ironing board and the sink."

Mrs. Sayre understood the diffidence of women who didn't mind coming to a meeting but who didn't want to lead one. She also recognized the feelings of those "who came to get a dinner." She had encountered these types since the early days in New Virginia, and she never was impatient with them.

Through her example, many Farm Bureau women gained the confidence they needed to carry out their goals, but they lacked training, and special courses were set up for them at the national, regional, and state levels. In 1951 the president and vice-president of the Associated Women and six representatives of four regions were appointed to the AFBF resolutions committee for the first time. Mrs. Sayre was no longer the only woman on the board, and while some women might have mourned the loss of that distinction, she rejoiced that more women finally were receiving their due.

Mrs. Charles Sewell, the administrative director of the Associated Women since the organization's beginning, retired in 1951. The general feeling was that she was irreplaceable, but Mrs. Sayre encouraged Miss Mary Roberts to accept the post and helped her in every possible way. Under the new system, Miss Roberts was a member of the Farm Bureau staff.

Speaking at regional meetings and training schools all over the country, Ruth Sayre explained the progress toward equality for women in the Farm Bureau. As she had said so many times before, "Problems do not have gender. There are not many problems that are solely masculine or feminine. The advantages of partnership lie in the fact that women are creators of public opinion. As part of the Farm Bureau, they can more effectively cooperate in the Farm Bureau program. They can strengthen its membership and its influence. They are important in building attitudes conducive to the understanding of farm problems."

In the spring of 1951 the Commission on Human Rights invited Ruth Sayre to sit on the platform at a large meeting Eleanor Roosevelt would address in Des Moines. She said, "I was to be the one woman on the platform besides Mrs. Roosevelt, and I decided the occasion called for a new hat. I bought a beauty with roses and doodahs—a spring hat. I woke up that morning to a blizzard, and I thought I shouldn't wear that hat with the roses, so I sadly put on an old, black felt. When I got to the meeting, Mrs. Roosevelt was wearing an old, black felt too."

Foreign travel was becoming a yearly habit for Mrs. Sayre, and in April 1951 she began a journey around the world that stemmed from an invitation to visit the women's institutes of Australia and New Zealand.

"My thrift instincts prompted me to keep right on going," she said, "as that first ticket was a good start."

She would visit seventeen countries in thirteen weeks, crossing the equator four times, losing a day of her life at the International Date Line, and trading a spring for two autumns. She estimated that she slept in fifty different beds, gave more than 100 speeches, drank gallons of tea, shook hundreds of hands, and "lived to tell the tale."

The first stop was Honolulu, where Home Demonstration people met her and took her on an auto tour of the city, including the beach at Waikiki and the Punch Bowl military cemetery, which brought a painful reminder of Dick Jacobs, Helen's first husband. After a breakfast with the Home Demonstration Council and some college representatives which featured native songs and dances, Mrs. Sayre departed wearing fifteen leis. She reflected that four hours were too little time to spend in Honolulu.

Her plane landed on Canton Island, a coral atoll in the Pacific, for refueling and took off again, but as dinner was being served on the plane, engine trouble was announced. The craft returned to Canton Island, where it stayed for two days and three nights.

"By then I was ready to write a book on Canton Island," Ruth Sayre said. "There is no vegetation, and all food and drinking water has to be brought in. There was nothing to do but sit near a fan and write letters." She also worried about the women who were planning her appearances in New Zealand, but the engine was repaired at last, and they flew on to Fiji and from there to Auckland, New Zealand.

"By the time I got there, all the flowers they had ready for me had wilted," she said. "They were very good about it. They had to cancel two days of meetings, but with Miss Kane's help (and she is a very capable and marvelous person) I managed to cover most of New Zealand in a sort of way. As you know, the country is two islands. We came in at Auckland and with only eight days—one of them a Sunday—I saw Wellington, Christchurch (the most English city I saw there), Dunedin (the most Scottish, and I told them there that one of my grandfathers was a Scot), and Rotorua, where I saw the Maoris sing and dance."

A typical day in New Zealand involved preparing a script for a radio broadcast, visiting correspondence schools peculiar to Australia and New Zealand, having tea with the Prime Minister, speaking to a women's meeting, addressing 400 women at lunch, making another broadcast, eating dinner, and taking a train to the next stop.

Her only complaint was, "They saw a good deal of me and heard a great deal from me, but I did not see enough of them or hear enough from them about what they are doing and what they think. I felt I had very little talk with the women themselves. I think in planning such trips in the future, it is equally as important for the person who goes to visit to learn and see and hear from the women as for you to give them whatever you have to say. The whole thing must be a two-way street. Otherwise you can't see the country through the eyes of the people who live there."

A seaplane took Mrs. Sayre to Sydney, Australia, and one of the women awaiting her there reported, "It was a rough passage from New Zealand with a long wait at Rose Bay because of the plane schedule. Mrs. Sayre was tired, but this was not apparent in her manner. We expected a tall, efficient women and were rather surprised to see a small, pleasant one dressed in a red suit, black toque, and fur. You can't be with Mrs. Sayre very long without sitting up and taking notice. She is a real person whose values are founded on basic principles."

The Australian press described Ruth Sayre as "speaking in a soft voice with sensitive, deft hands. She doesn't dramatize but makes world problems sound like naughty boys rather than fearsome bogeys. She makes one feel that we can and should cope with them. She has a good sense of humor and an easy and friendly manner, like a neighbor who has just dropped in for a chat. The simplicity with which she presents her subjects can come only from a thorough knowledge.''

In Tasmania she made broadcasts, visited area schools, spoke at several meetings, and planted a tree in honor of the celebration of fifty years of federation in the Commonwealth, which was the original reason for her trip as the guest of the Australian government.

"It rained and rained while I was planting the tree," she said, "and they held a big umbrella over me. I feel sure that tree will grow. At Dundas women were seated around me on the platform and at the back of me. The hall was full, and there were people peeking in through the doors and windows. Tasmania was more like England than any other part of the world I had seen.''

Lady Binney, Mrs. Sayre's hostess in Tasmania, writes from her present home in Essex, England, "She stayed with us in Tasmania when my husband was governor of that state, and we both found her quite charming, extremely intelligent, and immensely well-informed of the situations of the various societies of ACWW with their connections through agriculture with the UN. So much so, in fact, that my husband arranged for her to see our prime minister rather than the minister of agriculture, as we thought her brilliant brain would rather overwhelm him.''

Mrs. Sayre said of Lady Binney, "She will be a great addition on the executive council—is very enthusiastic," and was pleased when she went on to become president of ACWW.

Comments about Mrs. Sayre's Australian tour were universally positive: "Mrs. Sayre inspired an audience of over 1,200 in the Shire hall. Members had traveled as far as 360 miles and many would not be home before 10 p.m., but everyone who made the trip agreed it had been well worth making a special effort.''

Ruth Sayre told her listeners, "Americans are informal people. They don't give speeches, just talks.''

The day after the Shire hall "talk," an audience of 1,000 women listened to her speak after a delayed plane made her an hour late, and one of them said, "She is a real country woman who has all the qualities of good leadership, puts first things first, and has the ability to inspire all who hear her.''

Western Australia reminded her of California, and in South Australia, she said, "Here I got the feeling of outback, but I'm sure I

After a rough passage from New Zealand in 1951,
Mrs. Sayre landed with a smile at Sydney,
Australia.

never did really get out back, because no matter how far out back you go, there is still more outback.''

She learned from a country wife that salt sage grass contributes to the finest Merino wool and filed that fact away for Raymond. At Phillip Island, she saw Koala bears and penguins, and when she expressed the desire to see a kangaroo in its native habitat during another stop, her hosts suggested that they go to the zoo. She declined, saying she could do that at home, but in due course, she did see a leaping marsupial in the wild.

The Country Women of Australia concentrated on the maintenance of hostels for girls who must travel far from home for an education, and Ruth Sayre noted, "Their work is almost a community welfare thing and quite different from what we are doing in many other countries. It means that an immense amount of money is raised to carry on these projects, all voluntary contributions."

How were the contributors persuaded? Partially, at least, by the careful use of the money they gave. Ruth Sayre chuckled as she told this story: "A man had a gadget to sell at an agricultural show to squeeze juice out of a lemon. When he squeezed and squeezed, this would get every bit of juice from the lemon. He demonstrated this to farmers and their wives and said, 'If anyone can get out one more drop, I will give them a pound.' A little woman said, 'I'd like to try.' She squeezed and squeezed and got two drops out of the lemon. The salesman was so surprised that he said, 'Who on earth are you?' She answered, 'I'm the treasurer of my CWA.' "

Although Mrs. Sayre never complained about matters concerning her own comfort, her visit to Australia coincided with a fuel crisis, and she shivered, took cold baths, and ate cold food. She did express her disappointment that her audiences were all women. She had been accustomed to talking to men too. Also, she worried the whole time about leaving her attic in a mess, asking herself, "What if something should happen to me?"

She told Australian women what she had been telling American women for some time: "It is not enough for any woman to believe she has done her duty if she stays at home. She must have a broader horizon and keep the international pot from boiling over just as she must look after the pot on the stove in her own home."

Ruth Sayre realized that many of these women were exiles of a sort. To them, England was home. She thanked them for all their kindnesses to American soldiers during the war, noting that they had fed five million GIs, and she quickly grasped their problems: isolation, lack of library service, lack of education, low per capita income, and arid land.

The old problem of language differences surfaced, notably in a long conversation about air conditioning in which Ruth Sayre was talking about cooling and the Australian was talking about heating. It was easier to remember that a field was a paddock.

Parting from many new friends, Mrs. Sayre set off for London via Singapore, Cairo, and Cyprus. The sights of Singapore were an Oriental delight, but she was eager to get on to Cairo, where she would meet Alice, who was on leave from her duties on Cyprus.

Alice Sayre has said, "No one should ever go on a trip with Mother and think they are going to have a vacation!"

Ruth Sayre was photographed sitting on a camel with her hat on straight, her dress modestly covering her legs, and her purse threaded over one arm, but she was less eager to see the pyramids and the Sphinx than she was to learn what the rural women of Egypt were doing and thinking. The sight of them cutting grain with tiny blades tied to each of two fingers filled her with zeal to improve their lot.

The same interests would drive her on Cyprus, where she had planned to rest in Alice's home before going on to London. After showing her mother everything that could be seen in two days, it was Alice who needed a rest, and Ruth Sayre's mind was churning the plight of Cypriot peasant women, who were trapped in their class for life.

14

The International Mind

IN England in June 1951 Ruth Sayre observed that British farm organizations did not accept the women's institutes. There was no evidence of men and women working together, and she said, "The more I travel, the more I realize how women are or are not organized, and the more apparent becomes the need for developing a variety of organizations for women to help them learn how to work with men and their organizations."

While in London the working president of the ACWW addressed the National Federation of Women's Institutes of England and Wales, Jersey, Guernsey, and the Isle of Man. To emphasize the international thrust of her remarks, Ruth Sayre wore an Indian sari to speak to the 5,000 women gathered in Albert Hall.

"From where I stood, their faces looked like rows of white plates," she said.

Mrs. Sayre brought greetings from the rest of the five and a half million members of ACWW, particularly from those in New Zealand and Australia whom she had just visited, and she challenged her audience to address the complex problems of averting war and gaining peace and security. How? By developing the "international mind," which she defined as "knowing that a threat to peace and freedom in any part of the world is a threat to peace and freedom in all parts of the world. No man is an island. International-mindedness is knowing also how we can play our part in the world effectively and intelligently."

She urged the women to "learn the economic facts of life," to understand "the problems of production and consumption, world trade and distribution, population trends, and monetary and fiscal policies. For what will it profit a woman to be wise in the skill of bottling food and adept in the art of crafts if she lacks knowledge and understanding of the world in which she lives, and of the forces that are making her world what it is?''

Quoting a male who said, ''Luckily women don't go in for information, or if they give it, it is so incorrect as to be harmless,'' she countered with I. A. R. Wylie's comment, ''Women are no dumber than men. They couldn't be!'' then adding George Eliot's line from *Mill on the Floss,* ''Women are fools, of course they are. God Almighty made them to match men.'' Then came her own contention, ''We can all be more or less foolish according to how much pains we take to make ourselves intelligent and to count in what happens in our nation and the world.''

She questioned whether women were using their full power to prevent war, noting, ''There has been, on the part of women, almost an obsession with the goal of peace, existing at the same time with an unwillingness to take responsibility for doing those things which will make peace possible.''

Rejecting the suggestions that the five and a half million Country Women all sign a petition for peace to be sent to the United Nations and organize a day of worldwide prayer as ''too easy,'' Mrs. Sayre said, ''This is not enough—to sign a petition or to say a prayer and leave the rest to God. God expects us to do something for ourselves.''

She pointed out the importance of improving living standards in rural areas, saying, ''There is no doubt that empty stomachs and ignorance and poverty contribute to the tensions and frustrations that lead people to war. . . . The awakening consciousness of the people of the so-called economically underdeveloped countries is the most powerful single force shaping history today.''

Moving on to the lack of opportunity for rural children, Ruth Sayre cited specific situations like the fact that two-thirds of the children in Malaya received no education at all.

She stressed the importance of the new Technical Assistance program designed to help the people of underdeveloped countries find their own way to peace and stability.

''Country Women need especially to emphasize to the United Nations the fact that work among the women is highly important, as it reaches out to the whole family. This phase is too much neglected because it is more difficult. Entry into the home *can* be made and most easily through the kitchen. We need to point out the need for adult education programs for rural women, the ways in which the burdens of peasant women can be lightened by the introduction of simple improvements over primitive techniques in homemaking, the use of such devices as community mills for grinding corn, the distribution of chores among all of the family.''

Ruth Sayre made her point about the slow business of changing cultural habits and life patterns by saying, ''In a so-called highly developed country it is not easy to get a housewife to put a long handle on her mop if she has always gotten down on her hands and knees to scrub her floor. But if we can only bring half the world from the era of the sickle to the era of the scythe, we will have moved ahead a thousand years, and—more importantly—we will have dealt with one of the fundamental causes of war.''

Stripping the sentimental gloss from the term ''family of nations,'' she asked, ''Is it easy to live together in a family? Our own experiences teach us that there are many misunderstandings within a family. And we have only to look at our juvenile and domestic court records to see that families are not always as happy and united as the comparison would suggest. Even so, families *do* have many qualities advantageous to unity that the 'family of nations' does *not* have. The seventy sovereign nations have neither a single government, nor a common morality, nor a common tongue, nor a single standard of justice.''

What, then, could hold them together? Ruth Sayre's answer was ''friendship and understanding,'' and she went on to define what were glittering generalities in the minds of most: ''Understanding is something far more than information. It means three things: it means seeing other peoples, not as 'foreigners' or 'aliens' or 'governments,' but as human beings—living, working, thinking, loving, praying, suffering, dying. It means the ability to put oneself in the place of other people, to see things from *their* point of view.''

As Ruth Sayre ended her speech in Albert Hall, the rows of ''white plates'' became animated women rising to applaud. She had spoken their minds.

A writer for the British *Farmers Weekly* noted, ''I liked, too, the talk (as intimate as a fireside chat) given during the morning session of the Annual General Meeting of the Women's Institutes by another remarkable country woman, Mrs. Raymond Sayre (the president of ACWW). She has the perfect microphone technique. Nothing she says is startlingly new. What *is* new is the dash of realism with which she savours old ideas, making them seem fresh-minted.''

Evelyn Irons of the London *Evening Standard* wrote, ''Beneath the placid, plumpish exterior of Mrs. Sayre, mother of four and grandmother of three, smoulders the fiery spirit of a hot gospeller. Her mission—to wake women up; push them beyond the horizons of husband, home, and children; cram them with knowledge of world economics; and bully the war-torn world into peace and social betterment.

"On the platform she wears a pink straw boater with a green rose in front bought in Indianola, Iowa. 'My audience will at least remember my hats,' she observes, 'even if they don't remember anything else about me.' But there is nothing rosy about her words."

Evelyn Irons quoted Mrs. Sayre's comment on her early Farm Bureau days, "I talked at meetings with one baby in my arms and another beside me," then told of her life on the farm at Ackworth and how she planted 400 tulip bulbs the previous year and never saw them flower. The piece ended, "Mrs. Sayre gives the conventional answer when asked which of her two lives she prefers. 'I just can't wait to get home,' she says with evident sincerity. But I opine that she would not be pleased if her easygoing husband put his foot down and said, 'No more hot-gospelling around the world.' I have seen the glint in her eyes."

The Festival of Britain was going on while Ruth Sayre was in England, and Stella Bell and her husband John took their American guest to the two exhibition centers on the south bank of the Thames.

Mrs. Bell recalls, "In one of the big halls was a sort of Don Quixote figure on a horse with a mechanical hand patting himself on the back and a record repeating a little jingle, 'Give yourself a pat on the back, a pat on the back.' This tickled both Mrs. Sayre and my husband, and they started to laugh heartily, and in a few moments had set everyone else near us laughing. It was one of those spontaneous, happy moments that one does not forget."

Mrs. Sayre had not meant to visit France on this trip, but a UNESCO meeting was being held in Paris, and she joined the United States national commission there for two days, which gave her a chance to observe the French national elections.

"I was with friends who were strong supporters of de Gaulle," she said, "and they were certain their party would win, but the victory went to the middle-of-the-road faction. It was better so. De Gaulle was a dictator, and the only other party was Communist."

Before returning to Ackworth on July 1, Ruth Sayre had further obligations to both business and pleasure: speaking engagements in Canada, New York, and Chicago, and a visit with Helen and her family in Massachusetts. She was now fifty-five, but she took on her responsibilities with unflagging energy. As a Brisbane, Australia, journalist had observed, "She does not waste energy but understands how to keep her reserves while giving out the real things."

The stopover in Framingham was a special kind of renewal. Ruggie was delighted to see his Grandma, and Cindy was an adorable baby.

Ruth Sayre had started out three months before with sixty-six pounds of luggage: two medium-sized bags, a hat box, and a vanity case, and souvenirs had increased the weight. She considered it fortunate that memories weighed nothing.

Telling Raymond of the beautiful flight over the Alps with a clear view of mountains, rivers, large and small farms, castles, and towns, she said, "We ought to go to Europe together. There are so many wonderful things to see!"

He nodded, smiling. "Someday there'll be time."

The American press was interested in Mrs. Sayre's reactions to the world situation, and she told Lulu Mae Coe of the *Des Moines Register* that women everywhere were united in wanting peace, but they were doing too much wishful thinking and too little spadework on the subject.

The visit to Australia had made the Ackworth farm of 600 acres seem no bigger than a city block, but Ruth Sayre soon regained her American perspective, flying to the Carolinas, Michigan, and California to speak.

In Charlotte she talked about Germany, saying, "The Germans don't practice democracy in the home. That's the big problem. It's difficult for us to understand, since democracy is as common to the American as the air he breathes, but in Germany the man in each household is like a little Hitler, and the family comes to him requesting permission to do everything from baking the bread to planting the roses."

At Michigan State College, she told an ACWW convention, "If women really want peace in the world, they are going to have to leave home—mentally. . . . Oftentimes they are afraid to realize what they could achieve if they began to think and work on a national-international level.

"And where could women start? Inflation is a good spot. Women don't realize what they could do to stop inflation. They are buyers. Think how much they could do to hold down soaring prices if they would buy only essentials and put their extra money into bonds. They could start a passive boycott that might have startling effects."

There was praise for American women too in her comment that they were "more willing to stick their necks out in taking definite stands about issues in our government than British or Australian farm women," qualified with, "but they don't stick their necks out far enough."

Even as she spoke about past travels, Ruth Sayre was planning

In 1951 Ruth Sayre found a receptive audience at the Chicago meeting of the Associated Women of the AFBF.

another extensive trip. She had been invited to visit Africa in 1952, and as usual, she would make other stops along the way.

Working with Gertrude Dieken of the *Farm Journal* in Philadelphia, Mrs. Sayre was crystallizing the conclusions from her trip around the world in an article titled "FREEDOM FIRST, Peace Second," which was published in the October 1951 issue of the magazine. The piece brought heavy reader response and won the Freedoms Foundation Award.

The article began, "I have been around the word, and I am worried about women and peace. It seems to me that women are obsessed with peace, as if repeating this magic word will bring it to pass. And that is why I am worried. There *is* no magic way to peace. And it is not a simple thing nor a simple word. On the contrary, peace is a dangerous word—not to be used without thinking what we *mean*. You can have a kind of peace in jail!"

She observed that the Chinese word for peace means "rice in the mouth." French women regarded neutrality as peace, and a German woman was likely to say, *"Ohne mich,"* or, if war comes, "count me out."

Mrs. Sayre asked, "What kind of peace comes first?" and answered, "To me the only real peace is the kind that assures freedom, not only for me, but for everybody else. I know, as never before, what I as an American woman mean when I use those rather formal words, 'individual freedom.' "

Describing her travels in countries where some kinds of freedom had been sacrificed for peace-with-security, she analyzed the factors that form American freedom: "For one thing, we have a spirit to get things done. When we are faced with a problem, we say, 'Well, what can we do about it?' And we do something—soon. For us, the impossible only takes a little longer than the possible. Believe me, it's not that way everywhere. In many parts of the world, people seem so resigned to things the way they are. It's hard for an American to understand how they can go along so patiently, so hopelessly.

"Our American spirit, I believe, comes from being able to make free choices. We can decide how to spend our money, where to go into business, what business to go into. We can choose what kind of house we want to build (how big, how many windows), to whom we want to sell our wheat and cotton and how and when. Such free choice of millions of people is more likely to bring the right answer than the best of planned economies, in which a few men, no smarter than anyone else, make the decisions for the many."

She warned Americans against taking freedom for granted, saying, "When you stop valuing something, you're in danger of losing it."

Another American strength she identified was the belief in universal education leading to freedom of thought, and she said, "We take part in our educational system. Our public education is not handed us on a platter by the state. We have a say in our local affairs, and that, to me, is part of peace-with-individual-freedom."

Mentioning the absence of a class system as still another component of American freedom, Mrs. Sayre quoted a French visitor who said, "In the United States, everybody has a future." She added, "That may not, unfortunately, be true for every last person here, but at least we come closer to it than any other people."

She compared the lot of an American woman to that of a woman in Germany or on the island of Cyprus and said, "Of all the world's women, American women have the most freedom of individual choice: what to do with their lives, what to buy, what to read, what to do with their time, what to think . . . for over here, women are people. Our opinions and advice and counsel are welcomed, not only by our husbands, but also by our communities, our organizations, our government.''

Discussing American creature comforts, she said they existed because "free men have an incentive to produce and do it competitively," and they freed American women from the drudgery she had seen in other countries. She did, however, warn against the imposition of our standards of living on others, writing, "Those of us who have a lot shouldn't talk too much about it. I was told in no uncertain terms when interviewed on the radio in another country, 'Now, we don't want to hear about your American kitchens and your gadgets.' "

Mrs. Sayre pointed out the importance of realizing that other people "don't value the same things we do. We must only help people help themselves. . . . We must be more concerned that other nations have freedom to *make* choices than over what their choices are."

The conclusion was "Let's be realistic when we say we want peace. We really want it only one way—with freedom. And freedom comes first."

The year had passed so quickly, and its end was signaled, as usual, by the annual American Farm Bureau Federation convention, this time at the Stevens Hotel in Chicago.

Ruth Sayre came home to find John waiting beside the box of Christmas tree ornaments. The Yuletide season couldn't start officially until Mother arrived.

The Christmas cards, which now staggered Opal in the Ackworth post office, included a message from Mrs. Leslie Craig of Perth, Australia, that read, "You will never know how much good your visit did. You are doing a great job with ACWW, and we are all so proud of you."

A Norwegian woman wrote, "You have the gift of getting just the essentials and the very spirit of countries, nationalities, and events."

15

The Politics of Want and Plenty

EARLY in 1952 consumer reaction to high food prices amounted to an attack on the nation's farmers, and Ruth Sayre rallied the Farm Bureau women to the defense.

"We were not economists," she said, "but we were consumers as well as producers—consumers of industrial products, farm machinery, fertilizer, gas and oil, and household goods. We knew the problem from both sides, and we certainly were aware that inflation had reduced the purchasing power of the farmer's dollar too."

The Farm Bureau staff marshalled facts and figures on the issue, and rural-urban discussion groups met in the states and counties. Having attended rural-urban conferences for a dozen years, Mrs. Sayre was well acquainted with the nuances of relationship between town and country. She had, in fact, combined them in her own life, but she always said, "I married the farm."

Calling a press conference at the Mayflower Hotel in Washington, D.C., February 1, 1952, Ruth Sayre said, "Are farmers greedy? Are food prices too high? Are farm prices causing inflation? Are farmers getting rich? The American housewife thinks the answers to these questions are 'Yes!'

"The American farmer's wife says, 'Listen to our side of the story. We think food prices are lower than they used to be when compared with things required to earn food in the United States. Food prices are not high compared to other things the housewife buys. Between June 1950 and June 1951 the price of furnishings rose more than food prices did, but because the housewife buys food every day and doesn't buy household furnishings so often, she is not as conscious of the price rise going on in the rest of the economy.

"The farm housewife believes the city housewife should realize she is feeding her family better than she used to—buying more food and higher quality food. The farmer gets a very small share of the consumer's food dollar."

Mrs. Sayre introduced Allan Kline, and the Farm Bureau president said, "The consumer must not expect to get food prices that penalize the producer. Food is a bargain. Consumers are spending a small portion of their income on food."

Kline warned that price fixing would put agriculture in a straitjacket, and Ruth Sayre added, "If we do not want price controls, we must make up our minds to voluntarily curb our buying. Price alone is not the issue."

At a Producers Commission annual meeting in Sioux City, Iowa, Mrs. Sayre said, "We must help the urban consumer understand farm problems. They don't realize the farmer's problems. They don't realize the farmer's costs."

Taking their cue from Ruth Sayre, Farm Bureau women were passing the word along on this issue and many others. Allan Kline commented, "The Farm Bureau women are getting so they are not afraid to deal with issues."

The year 1952 was to be one of the busiest of Ruth Sayre's life, and if she had not been fully present with her husband when she *was* at home, he might have been less obliging about her frequent absences.

Years later, she said, "Sometimes I wonder if I should have gone off as much as I did, but I console myself that it's not how much time you spend with your family, but what you do with them when you *are* there that counts."

Laura Lane observes, "I do know that Mrs. Sayre's husband would have had to be a strong character himself not to resent the attention that was paid to her during a number of years when she was really a world figure."

In May Ruth Sayre attended a two-day training conference of the Associated Women of the AFBF in Salt Lake City, enjoying a visit with Roger Fleming at the sessions, and, at the end of that month, she received Parsons College's Community Development Award for "her outstanding achievements as a leader with rural women's organizations in the communities of Mid-America and throughout the world."

June was a month filled with honors. At the 1952 commencement exercises of Iowa State College, Ruth Sayre received her second honorary Doctor of Laws Degree for "her leadership of five and a half million

Being at home on the farm near Ackworth was
a rare treat for Ruth Sayre in 1952.

rural women and work for world understanding capably, gracefully, and
with unassuming humility, thus endearing herself to the women."

Gertrude Dieken saluted "Dr. Sayre" in the *Farm Journal,*
writing, "In spite of all her world work, she doesn't neglect her home
work. . . . She keeps a good home; raised an outward-looking family.
She *gave*—time, strength, real mental work."

Also in June Mrs. Sayre was invited to the annual convention of
the American Home Economics Association in Atlantic City, where she
and Dr. Lillian Gilbreth, subject of *Cheaper by the Dozen,* were to
receive honorary memberships.

There were times, however, when the family had to come first. The

Sayres were now grandparents for the fourth time, and their daughters and other grandchildren were coming home for a reunion that would include getting acquainted with Ann, born to Bill and Ruthann Sayre May 5.

Louise Rosenfeld of Iowa State College accepted the Home Economics Assocation honor for Mrs. Sayre, and Florence Fallgatter, president of the Association, said, "Mrs. Sayre has contributed much to the world's homes—specifically in the building of friendly feelings among women all over the world who have a common interest in homes."

Because of her position as president of the Associated Women of the American Farm Bureau Federation, Ruth Sayre was wooed by both political parties in this presidential election year. Bertha Adkins, executive director of the Women's Division of the Republican Party, wrote, "Your organization is doing a splendid job of stimulating political activity." Shortly thereafter, Mrs. Gilford Mayes, assistant chairman of the Republican National Committee, sent a ticket for National Convention sessions at the Stockyards Auditorium in Chicago, and Mrs. Sayre also was invited to gatherings preceding the July 7 opening of the Republican Convention.

She declined the pre-convention invitations, needing to be with Helen. Soon after arriving at the farm with Ruggie and Cindy, Helen mentioned that a mole on her back was being irritated by her clothing. They went to Des Moines to have it removed, and laboratory tests indicated malignancy. Further surgery was performed, and the family then felt the cautious hope that all would be well, but they needed to be together as long as possible after this frightening experience.

India Edwards, vice-chairman of the Democratic National Committee, personally invited Mrs. Sayre to Chicago for the Democratic National Convention beginning July 21, but a speech in Louisiana was scheduled for that date, and Mrs. Sayre sent word that she would arrive later.

Knowing that she represented Farm Bureau women of widely diverse political opinions, Ruth Sayre attended both conventions as an observer, showing seemingly equal enthusiasm. She did, however, like Ike. Franklin Delano Roosevelt's New Deal had not bought the Iowa farmer's affections or continuing support for his party, and in any case, Ruth Sayre came from a long line of Republicans. Her vote, which would be by absentee ballot because she would be out of the country on election day, was a well-kept secret at both Chicago conventions, but somehow her recollections are all Republican.

Breakfasting with Mamie Eisenhower at the Blackstone Hotel, Ruth Sayre found the general's lady to be most gracious. She said,

"Mrs. Eisenhower was told that I was a farm woman, and she talked about the corn Ike planted in their small garden in Paris. I also talked to Ike and quizzed him on farm questions. I decided he would be in sympathy with the Farm Bureau. However, I refused to be a member of the Citizens for Eisenhower National Committee because the Farm Bureau was nonpartisan, and many of its members were Democrats."

Seated in the balcony of the Stockyards Auditorium, Mrs. Sayre kept careful tally as the states called our their preference: Dwight D. Eisenhower or Robert A. Taft. She could not see the features of the people on the floor, but she observed that the press section was as large as the space for official delegates. She also noted that the women were well dressed with furs and pearls much in evidence, and a plank in the party platform stating that farmers were for freedom, not government control, pleased her greatly.

When the political conventions were over, Ruth Sayre had a short respite from constant travel and spent hours working in her garden. While her hands were busy weeding, her mind was occupied with coming events, and from time to time she sat back on her heels and thought of Helen. The health of her firstborn was a worrisome matter.

In early September Ruth Sayre donned navy lace to address the annual dinner of the Missouri Home Economics Extension Club Council at Columbia. She told them that other countries of the world had nothing quite as good as the Land-Grant College and Extension Service for meeting the needs of rural people.

"American women have progressed from the 'family mind' to the 'national mind,' " she said, "but if we are to gain world peace, we must learn the 'international mind.' "

Soon after John began his senior year of high school, Ruth Sayre departed for London, where she would spend five days before proceeding to India and Pakistan.

Speaking at an executive meeting of the ACWW, she defined the purpose of the organization thus, "First: it is a voice for country women in international councils. Second: it is a movement to improve the lot of country women. Third: it is an association to promote goodwill, a fellowship to build a bridge of understanding, a window to the world that widens the horizon of country women."

In reference to the first purpose, she said, "We have to recognize our limitations in acting as a voice for country women in international

In the summer of 1952, Helen and her children, Cindy and Ruggie, came home to Ackworth for a visit.

councils. . . . We are rural, a country women's organization, and therefore we do not have competence in every field. In three things we have competence: in the field of agriculture; in the field of home, family, and community life; and in the field of adult education for rural women. . . . We are not all things to all people. We can only be the voice for country women in these particular fields, but I am not sure that we always recognize our limitations.

"One limitation is that we do not have enough trained leaders in ACWW to speak in all the councils, everywhere, all the time." She noted that this was perfectly natural, as country women had been burdened with home and family and had had less opportunity for education and leisure than urban women.

She saw another limitation in the fact that "we still do not know what the individual member thinks on international matters. . . . What is it that women want most in the world? They want peace, they tell me in every country I go to, yet there is scarcely an organization that has a resolution concerning our problems which must be solved if we are going to have peace. . . . The greatest need in our organization today is to inform the individual member about problems that have to do with international affairs. They know national affairs and are beginning to take part in them, but very few know anything about the international problems. I know why. Because they are difficult, and they are complex."

She talked about the world food problem, saying, "The answer is that we have to help every country to produce more so that they can help to feed themselves.

"There is the whole problem of world trade, a terribly difficult and complex one, but if the women of the world really want peace, they will have to put their minds to the problem of trade. We started fifteen years ago in my own state trying to educate our members to the problems of world trade. We talked about internationalism and the larder shelf, starting with the things people know. We said, 'Here you are, using tea from one country, spices and sugar from others.' Then we talked about trading with other countries. We took it step by step, trying to make them understand. I have been very proud of that fact, for, because of that background, when the problem came up of restricting Danish Blue Cheese from coming in, our women were not for it. They understood the restriction was not for the good of Denmark, not for the good of the world. Because we had led them little by little, there was understanding of a world problem at a time when it became necessary to take a position on it."

Mrs. Sayre made a plea for the education of the ACWW membership in the facts and figures of international economic problems, saying, "They certainly affect the peace of our world."

Improving the life of country women in the underdeveloped nations through the UN's Technical Assistance programs and the British Colombo Plan was another major point in her address, and she told the women, "There are five things you can do: 1. Support in your own organizations and countries policies that will help to make this kind of program possible. 2. Help to promote understanding both among your members and the public of what the situation is and what the needs are. 3. Interest qualified people in working and teaching in underdeveloped areas. It is not easy to get people to go out and do these jobs. They cannot be well paid, but you might be able to help. 4. Help in specific projects in sending things to groups through the UNESCO coupon plan. Seven countries are now contributing in this way. 5. Help to get women's groups organized in these countries in consultation with the Food and Agriculture Organization or on your own."

The business of promoting goodwill and understanding was never more necessary nor more difficult, she said, "The world is full of tensions, and we have a great deal more nationalism than we had before. . . . We have many new nations, and each nation is thinking of itself. If you could draw vertical lines on a map of the world representing all the countries and horizontal lines representing the tensions of people on the top who have more and people at the bottom who do not have and are therefore trying to push up—if you imagine a map of the world crisscrossed by all these lines, each one bursting and pushing one way or another—you have some idea of the tremendous tensions abroad in the world today.

"When someone builds a dam, they build a spillway so the water doesn't break the dam. That I think you can do. You can build those little spillways to relieve the pressure so that tensions do not break out in war or revolutions."

One of the spillways she named was building a respect for differences—not tolerance, but respect. She said, "One of the great impressions that I have is that we are so very different. I used to give talks saying the people of the world are all alike. Now I consider that a great mistake—a mistake because it makes the job seem easy. . . . You have to know that coming together is a long, difficult matter which calls for much respect, unselfishness, and tolerance."

Another spillway she described was faith in the United Nations, and she said, "Almost everywhere people have become discouraged about the UN. They are very frustrated, very confused, and they say it isn't going to work." Ruth Sayre begged the women of the Executive

Council to say, "We haven't given it time to work yet. . . . We have only barely begun."

Mrs. Sayre always aimed for an upbeat close when she spoke, and this time she urged faith "in the ability of people of the world to work together, faith in ourselves and faith in human beings," finishing with a challenging stanza from a poem by Christopher Fry that began, "Thank God your time is now."

After attending a party given in her honor by Madame Subandrio, wife of the Indonesian Ambassador to England, Ruth Sayre prepared to fly to New Delhi, but first she wanted to buy a tea cozy. English friends forestalled the purchase, knowing that the Handicrafts Committee planned to give her a powder blue linen tea cozy embroidered in white.

In India one of Mrs. Sayre's first acts was to present UNESCO coupons purchased with money from the women of the Indiana Farm Bureau and the North Carolina State Agricultural Association to Janta College in Alipore near New Delhi.

Although Janta was called a college, actually it was a training center where farmers were prepared for rural leadership with UNESCO assistance, and the coupons from American farm women were earmarked for a small generating plant, a weaving machine, and a small knitting machine.

Ruth Sayre had said earlier, "Not a single technical program is trying to reach the women. You will never raise the standard of living, you will never change the attitudes, you will never increase production until you get to the women and interest them."

Visiting one of the 305 Indian villages receiving UNESCO aid, Mrs. Sayre was met by all the men of this community of 120. She arrived in a wagon pulled by bullocks, and in spite of the stench and the heat, she managed to look fresh in a dress with three-quarter sleeves, a hat, and pearls without excessive use of the woven fan she carried. Walking beneath an arch of green leaves erected in her honor, she smiled at the Indian Boy Scouts who stood at attention. Surprised that no women had greeted her, she was even more surprised that none appeared before the platform from which she was to speak.

"What do you say to a large group of people sitting in an open space who don't know your language?" she asked herself, realizing that the people didn't know who she was or why she was there. Pressing her palms together, she attempted the Indian greeting, *"Namaste!"* Then, she said, "I tried to make it clear that American farm women were concerned that they should have the opportunity for education."

The women, to whom she could have spoken from the heart, were crowded into the hot, tiny rooms of the mud huts that ringed the village well, though a few had crept to the edge of the crowd with covered faces. It occurred to Ruth Sayre that an Indian man was more

*Boy Scouts welcomed Ruth Sayre to their village
in India with an arch of honor in 1952.*

likely to mourn the loss of an ox than that of a wife. An ox was harder to
replace. She must put even stronger emphasis on her belief that "The
progress of a country can be measured by the level to which its women
have been raised."

In spite of the language barrier, she tried to relate to the Indian experience, and her audience felt it. The minister of education responded
warmly to her remarks, and the villagers accorded her their sign of
friendship and respect, a red dot on the forehead. After the formalities,
she ate and drank with the villagers, upsetting her digestion, but in true
Buxton style, she kept that secret well.

At last she saw some of the women, who were learning the
alphabet in an afternoon class. The men would study in the same room
at night. She said, "I tried to explain that we were interested in what
they were doing in education, and we had an organization trying to
help women improve—that I was a mother with children who went to
school."

Watching an Indian woman drawing water from the well in a clay jar, Ruth Sayre remembered her own water-carrying days in New Virginia, and when she visited the polio ward of an Indian hospital, she was reminded of her own work with the American Infantile Paralysis Foundation.

Back in New Delhi, Mrs. Sayre dined with Madame Pandit, Nehru's sister, and paid a visit to United States Minister Chester Bowles and his wife. Of Bowles she said, "He is no stuffed shirt, and he is very well liked in India."

The heat continued to be oppressive, and Mrs. Sayre was told that people worked in the 100-degree heat "because taking a nap made them feel worse."

Not knowing the customs, she wondered why she was expected to "stay and stay" at a tea when she was tired and wanted to leave. It finally occurred to her that others were feeling the same way, but she was the guest of honor, and good manners required that they stay until she left.

Before leaving India, Mrs. Sayre visited with Emma Harned, a former Simpson College student, who was married to a deputy to the American ambassador. Then, with a warm invitation to the Indian women to attend the 1953 ACWW Triennial in Toronto, Ruth Sayre was off to Karachi.

In Pakistan a strong organization of women—the All Pakistan Women's Association—seemed more than ready to join the ranks of the Associated Country Women of the World. Its president was Begum Liaquat Ali Khan, and an American woman doing home economics work in Pakistan took Ruth Sayre to meet her.

Mrs. Sayre said, "As we drove in, a door opened revealing a picture of the Ali Khan as big as life in the entry. It took my breath away."

The problems of Pakistan, she discovered, included an acute shortage of teachers and colleges for women; also inadequate nursing services for the widespread malnutrition, tuberculosis, and malaria in the country.

Begum Liaquat Ali Khan, widow of the prime minister, had torn away the veil of purdah, and she was responsible for establishing a school in Karachi, which she invited Ruth Sayre to visit. The Pakistani leader told Mrs. Sayre that the most lasting and significant achievement of the All Pakistan Women's Association was the creation among women of a new individual, social, and national sense of responsibility.

The women of Pakistan definitely were ready to put on the "international mind," Ruth Sayre thought, issuing another invitation to the Toronto Triennial. Recruiting Country Women was as natural for her as breathing.

16

Other Continents

AT Beirut Ruth Sayre reflected that she had been more impressed by India than she was by the Middle East, but of course she had seen more of India.

The next stop was Cairo, and Egypt was in turmoil over the dissolution of King Farouk's rule. Because the streets were unsafe, Ruth Sayre did not venture outside her hotel, but she consoled herself that she had "done" Egypt with Alice. In the morning she would fly to Nairobi and really experience the Dark Continent.

The East Africa Women's League had planned a conference of the constituent societies of ACWW in Nairobi, where Mrs. Sayre would be the guest of Lady Wilson, president of Kenya's equivalent to the Women's Institute.

Mrs. E. D. Hughes, an architect who was president of the East Africa Women's League, gave a garden party to honor delegates to the conference, and the guests wore spectacular clothes worthy of Ascot. Mrs. Sayre, "attired smartly in navy blue *broderie anglaise* with a matching hat ornamented with small flowers," mingled with the bishops of Mombasa and Uganda and any number of lords and ladies. This being a state occasion, she also wore three strands of pearls, earrings, and a brooch.

A sight-seeing safari to the Amboseli wildlife refuge twenty-five miles from Nairobi gave Ruth Sayre the opportunity to admire the lush countryside of mountains, lakes, and waterfalls; the profusion of flowers; and the breathtaking sight of hundreds of flamingos on a game reserve lake.

At the camp a fire was built to keep the wild animals away, but when the delegates were shown to individual tents, Mrs. Sayre fervently wished that she had a tent mate. It would help to have someone to talk and laugh with when the wild things made their night sounds.

As she was leaving the camp with Mrs. Claude Anderson and Mrs. Harold Williams of Northern Rhodesia, their car was blocked by a large rhinocerous. According to an East African newspaper report, "The animal peered in the direction of the car with one paw extended, but decided against taking action and waited for Mrs. Sayre and her party to make the next move. Unfortunately, they were unable to do this, as the car had stalled. The only method of escape was for someone to get out and push. With the rhino only a few yards away, Mrs. Williams performed this bold feat and, gathering the strength of ten, mobilized the vehicle. Mrs. Sayre remained quite calm, but she says she will be satisfied if her encounters with rhino in future are confined to the American screen!" Immediately after the rhino incident, the car had to dodge four elephants.

There were other terrors in the city. Although the Mau Mau uprisings were just beginning, the presence of an anti-European movement was quite apparent. Kenyatta, the leader, knew how to appeal to the savagery and witchcraft in the Kikuyu people, whose common language was a version of Swahili. Ruth Sayre's hosts told her that the language of the Kikuyu was the first thing a farmer taught his wife when she arrived in Kenya, but the Africans did not teach it to their women.

Mrs. Sayre was received graciously in white African homes and usually was assigned to a guest house away from the main house. She said, "I couldn't venture out at night alone, and I was a little fearful all alone and away from the big house."

She could sense what the black people were feeling as she observed the custodial attitude of the white Africans toward them. Her hosts carried the "white man's burden" with a sense of *noblesse oblige*, treating the blacks like little children, and Ruth Sayre could not bring herself to approve of their take-care rule. Surely the black Africans yearned for self-government—what human being did not?

Speaking with Mrs. Basil Price, the leader of a delegation from the Federation of Women's Institutes of Southern Rhodesia who had toured Kenya before the conference opened, Mrs. Sayre learned that members of the East Africa Women's League were working in an emergency canteen for troops called up to fight the Mau Mau threat at night and working in their offices and business during the day. They were responding to the needs of their country in their own way.

Eager to learn the results of the American presidential election,

Ruth Sayre hurried to a bulletin board outside the United States Information Service building in Nairobi. African friends helped her celebrate the transformation of General Eisenhower to President Eisenhower.

In Bulawayo, where she began an eleven-day visit to Southern Rhodesia, Ruth Sayre told reporters, "Most of the women in the world are country women."

To the women gathered at the Hillside Women's Institute, she said, "Women should never underestimate what they can do as individuals with a great idea. But they must be informed about world economic affairs as well as have enthusiasm. They should come to grips with the economic facts of life so they can understand the causes and not just talk about the effects." She noted that the basis of life is spiritual, and "the job we have to do is to restore our own souls to dignity, to belief, and to conscience."

Suggesting that the women of Africa could promote understanding by preparing pamphlets on their lives and work, she said, "The eyes of the world are on Africa today, for it is the meeting point between East and West, and people want to know how the racial problems are solved."

Where she might have scolded, she encouraged, and the Rhodesian press took her remarks in the constructive spirit with which they were spoken. Many of the women who heard Ruth Sayre speak traveled more than 100 miles to reach the institute in Bulawayo. Other women's institutes were waiting for her in Gwelo.

Besides the African women of British and Dutch descent, Ruth Sayre met the women of primitive tribes in jungle villages. She said, "I crawled through the low door of a hut to visit a woman sitting among domestic animals. She had three stones for cooking in the middle of the floor and no chimney. Her husband had other wives, as many as he could afford, and their huts were nearby. It was hard to explain ACWW to a woman like this, and I had to rely on the principle I learned many years before in the Irish Grove school district—begin where you are with what you have."

Ruth Sayre was the first member of ACWW ever to address women's groups in South Africa. When her plane landed at Cape Town, the welcoming party of seventeen included one man, F. A. Murray Louw, a wine farmer from Durbanville who was married to the president of the Cape Town Circle. The Louws took her to their country home, Vier Landen, where the gardens were at their best in mid-November.

Always interested in flowers, Mrs. Sayre enjoyed another garden tour with Mrs. P. J. Olivier, wife of the administrator of the Cape, who introduced her to the Cape's official flower, the wild Protea with spectacular, spiny blooms.

On the Monday after her Friday arrival, Ruth Sayre addressed a public meeting in the Pearl Town Hall, telling a mixed audience of men and women, "Study without action is futile, but action without study is fatal!"

Admittedly defensive about the apartheid problem, *Hearth and Home,* the official organ of the Cape Province Women's Agricultural Association, commented, "We deem it fortunate for Mrs. Sayre to visit South Africa at a time when, in the assemblies of the world, attention is sometimes brilliantly focused on our affairs. . . . It would be impolite on our part even to suggest a line of approach to our problems to a visitor whose intellectual integrity is so universally acknowledged and whose record of service has left its mark in so many countries of the world. What we do welcome in this respect, however, is the presence of Mrs. Sayre as a trained observer. . . . We appreciate the awareness that the basic attitude of a visitor is one of fairness to all."

Ruth Sayre responded with a discussion of tension barriers, saying, "Before the first World War, there were only about seven powers among whom serious tension could exist. Today, there are no less than sixty-four of these national groups, which have been born out of the conflict of two major wars." She spoke of fundamental differences among the nations, drawing her examples from countries far removed from South Africa. This lessened the emotional charge that would have obscured her meaning had she hit closer to home.

She opened the annual congress of the South African Women's Agricultural Union at Bloemfontein and spoke to the Federation of Women's Institutes of Natal, Zululand, Pondoland, and East Griqualand at Maritzburg, saying, "There is a great desire for international peace, but international problems have to be solved by people where they live with what they have. The problems of the world will be solved by people in their own homes and communities."

In Maritzburg she came close to spelling out the problems she saw as a "trained observer," saying, "In South Africa there are the problems of the East meeting West, of the many different races, in the great undeveloped human and material resources. I know of no other state that contains so many real, basic problems, but the way in which they are solved will not only help to make peace in South Africa but will help to forward peace all over the world."

Speaking to the Transvaal Women's Agricultural Union in Pretoria, she said, "We no longer have physical frontiers, but the hazards of the world today are spiritual, mental, and moral. A new kind of pioneer woman is needed in the world today. South Africans love their country, take pride in it, and have great faith in its future. I am particularly struck by the fact that the people here are a religious people who believe in more than material things."

Ruth Sayre flew from South Africa to London, arriving two days later than planned because of delayed planes and missed connections. Stella Bell says, "A pleasant programme had been arranged, including a short weekend at an English country house party, and telephones were red hot as we phoned the airlines, the hostesses, postponing, then canceling, then rearranging.

"Late Sunday afternoon, Mrs. Sayre had arrived safely, if tired. When I met her at the hotel, she was clutching a great armful of Proteas in bud. They are very heavy, and she had kept them with her all the way from South Africa, in and out of several countries, on and off planes, watching that they did not get left behind. She said, 'For goodness sake, take these and put them in water and bring them to the office next week!' There were moments when she longed to ditch them, but they were a gift to be brought to London to ACWW to bloom for weeks, and if you are Ruth Buxton Sayre, you don't lightly abandon a gift because plans have gone wrong and the gift has become a physical burden."

Ruth Sayre was interested in hearing how Mrs. Puleston Davies of Wales and Mrs. Janet Jury of Sussex had fared on their ten-week visit to the United States.

Mrs. Jury reported, "One girl explained rather painstakingly, rather as if I were a South Sea Islander, that they used tractors for some simple farm job. I think she was just going to tell me what a tractor was when I murmured that we used tractors for that job too."

With a wry smile, Mrs. Sayre noted that the concept of the "international mind" still needed work in her native land, but she was pleased that the English women had discovered "the Americans are just the same as ourselves. They have the same problems."

She flew home in time for the thirty-fourth annual American Farm Bureau Federation convention in Seattle, where she refused to allow her name to be presented for reelection as president of the Associated Women. Her successor was Mrs. Charles De Shazo of Virginia.

Reading the order of service in the traditional candle-lighting ceremony symbolizing love, courage, understanding, righteousness, patience, and faith on December 7, the first day of the conference, Ruth Sayre had a few qualms about what would happen to the Associated Women when Allan Kline left the AFBF presidency. He had given them free rein to operate while holding them accountable for the results of their actions.

On December 9 Ruth Sayre delivered the farewell address that

Roger Fleming remembers so well, "A Farm Woman Views the World." She offered impressions, she said, because "I am not one who believes that a short visit enables one to truly have a complete and comprehensive picture of a country."

She said that her African travels were paid for by the ACWW, "but my travel to India I paid for myself because I wanted to be free to find out and see things for myself."

What did she see? First, "The rest of the world is not in the image of America. To understand the people of the countries I visited, you have to look through their eyes. In India the people do not live as we live."

A different life-style was easier to understand than a different way of thinking, Mrs. Sayre found, and she observed, "The religion of India fosters a spirit of resignation and fatalism . . . a feeling of acceptance of things as they are."

Even so, she said, "India is ready to make some progress. For the first time in 200 years, the people feel they are free." After two centuries of British colonial rule, the Indian government was making land reforms (taking over the land and renting it back to the farmers on ninety-nine–year leases) and progressing in community development, literacy programs, and improved production through the use of better agricultural tools, seeds, and insecticides.

She spoke of Indian cooperation with the United States Technical Cooperation Administration programs and the five Ford Foundation training centers in India, and then came the candid comments of the observer who had paid her own way, "It seems to me that the TCA community programs are attempting to move too fast. On the other hand, I was told that if we don't sponsor these programs on a large scale, the Communists will move in.

"There are several things wrong with the US/TCA program in my opinion. First, I don't believe many of them are really technical assistance programs. Second, they are moving too fast and they are raising the expectations of the Indian people too high. If the expectations are not met, people will become discouraged and lose faith in the programs. Third, you can't change the attitudes of people as quickly as the technical experts hope to. Fourth, not a single technical assistance program has been developed to reach the women, and the only way you can succeed in a venture of this kind is to enlist the women. Fifth, there is a great danger that too much American aid will kill the Indian initiative. Sixth, there is danger in trying to impose our pattern of culture on the Indian people. They don't want to be like Americans, and it is not a case of envy of what we have. They want and like their own culture.

Seventh, there is the difficulty of securing American technicians who are really prepared to do the job. It is really a missionary job. We have some technicians over there who should not be there.''

Moving on to impressions of Africa, Mrs. Sayre said, ''In Africa you have all the problems of the world multiplied 100,000 times. Their problems are more intense; they are more critical.''

She identified those problems as the many political divisions that constituted barriers to trade, the struggle between East and West and the further struggle between the West and Communism, racial tensions, and competition for the rich but undeveloped natural resources of the continent: cobalt, sisal, uranium, gold, copper, and manganese. ''Africa is sensitive,'' she said, ''Africa is sitting on a volcano.''

She spoke of the native women of Africa, saying, ''Something has to be done about them if anything is to be done about Africa. The African woman is a human being a long, long way from you and me, but her freedom and ours, her progress and ours, are bound together.''

Relinquishing her national office, Ruth Sayre reaffirmed her international outlook, saying, ''What happens in these countries is of great concern to us. It is not enough to make America strong. We have to be concerned with what is happening in these other parts of the world. We must realize that there are comparatively few white people in the world, only one-third of the population. We have a responsibility to help gain freedom for the natives of these countries without revolution.

''Second, we must do everything we can to help the underdeveloped countries to help themselves. We must have technical assistance programs that are really such programs. We must develop mutual trade, even though at times it may be at our expense. Third, the ideal of freedom is the only one that might hold the world together. It is the only ideal that people have in common and will give loyalty to— that man must be freed. We must hold our faith in that ideal and never let that light grow dim.''

Her listeners in the huge sanctuary of Seattle's First Presbyterian Church rose to applaud, and Ruth Sayre knew that they would act as well. The Associated Women already had voted to cooperate with UNESCO in additional projects in India. Acknowledging the applause, she reflected that it had been a long road from New Virginia to Seattle.

Ruth Sayre's Christmas greeting to her friends around the world in 1952 was a Raphael Madonna and Child inscribed, ''May your good deeds continue to bring happiness and your good works bring us all a little nearer to peace on earth—goodwill to men.''

Goodwill from everywhere poured into the post office at Ackworth. A German woman wrote, ''You know that you have many good friends in this country who always are thankful for all the helping you have given in the first time, 1948. Nobody will forget this.''

Miriam Stewart wrote from Natal, ''I have learnt much from you. I have referred to you often and even used your words on my Christmas greeting.''

17

Passing the Torch

ON January 15, 1953, Ruth Sayre spoke at the Producers Livestock Commission Company annual meeting in Sioux City, Iowa, and "it was the worst day for an annual meeting in the history of the Producers. The blinding blizzard was so bad that fewer than 100 people were able to attend." Mrs. Sayre had bested blizzards before, and she told her meager audience, "We must help the urban consumer understand farm problems."

A movement was in progress to secure Eleanor Roosevelt's former position in the United States delegation to the UN for Ruth Sayre. Louise Rosenfeld, then assistant director of Home Economics at Iowa State College, wrote to President-elect Eisenhower urging Mrs. Sayre's appointment, "If you desire a woman of keen intellect, leadership qualities, great vision, experiences which touch into the individual lives and families and which broaden out to include the families of the world, a person with the greatest of interest in doing everything possible to bring understanding between the nations and a person who has great knowledge regarding the problems of peoples of other lands and who is a student of continuous learning, you have such a person in Mrs. Raymond Sayre. I trust every consideration may be given to her for this most important appointment."

Iowa U.S. Senator Guy Gillette, a Democrat, supported the appointment, but Dwight D. Eisenhower would have other plans for Mrs. Sayre which would be revealed in due course.

The February 1953 issue of the *Iowa Bureau Farmer* noted, "You often hear an outstanding Farm Bureau leader, whether at township, county, state, or national levels, referred to as 'Mr. Farm Bureau.' Our nomination for 'Mrs. Farm Bureau' is Mrs. Raymond Sayre, the Warren County, Iowa, woman who stepped down in December as president of the Associated Women of the American Farm Bureau Federation. She is still head of the Associated Country Women of the World.''

Mrs. Farm Bureau was busy preparing for the National Farm Institute in Des Moines, where she would join Ezra Taft Benson on the speaker's platform.

Her correspondence continued to be heavy, and a typical letter over her signature regretted that she could not attend a February meeting of the Council on Rural Health in Roanoke because she had a UNESCO meeting in New York on that date. Her communications were brief, pleasant, and to the point.

Ruth Sayre explored a new interest in 1953, becoming involved with the Farm Film Foundation, a nonprofit institution dedicated to creating better understanding between rural and urban Americans through audiovisual education.

As a member of the Town and Country Commission of the Methodist church, Mrs. Sayre was not bashful about pointing out that a world-need topic ignored the problems of domestic producers. She asked for a more realistic approach and less narrow implications.

A 1953 photograph of Ruth Sayre in coat and hat carrying her purse and a suitcase was captioned, ''Going somewhere?'' This year, at least, she would not leave her own continent, but she would be on the move.

In May Mrs. Sayre became associated with the American Friends Service Committee Institute of International Relations, and she would attend its June conference in Wichita.

Her article on the journey through Africa, India, and the Middle East, ''A Farm Woman Looks at the World,'' appeared in the May 1953 issue of the *Farm Journal,* drawing interested response from the magazine's readership.

John was graduated from high school in 1953, and he requested a trip with his parents as a graduation gift. They set out in a new dark green Pontiac Chieftain, and John says, ''After the Model T, my parents always had green cars.''

They toured historic places in the eastern United States; visited Raymond's first army post at Fort Monroe, Virginia; saw the sights of New York City and Washington, D.C.; and wound up in Framingham, Massachusetts, for a visit with Helen and her family.

The ACWW Triennial in Toronto was fast approaching, and after Ruth Sayre stepped down from the presidency, she planned to spend some time with Raymond in Mexico, where he had a meeting.

Each Triennial had its own special challenge, and the seventh at Toronto, which would be the largest since the 1936 meeting in Washington, was based on the theme, "How Can the Country Woman as an Individual and Through Her Society Take a More Active Part in International Work?"

As the women met in the Convocation Hall of the University of Toronto, they formed a bright, international collage: lace bonnets from the Netherlands, brilliant saris from India, skirts of woven stripes from Finland. Ruth Sayre had a particularly warm greeting for the women of nations represented for the first time: Japan, Lebanon, Pakistan, and Egypt.

Dorothy McGrigor, an old friend from Essex, England, asked Mrs. Sayre, "And how does your husband fare?"

"Very well," said Ruth, "I have told him he must eat cold."

Stella Bell says, "I could have been very sad at Toronto, for one's first president holds a very special place in one's life, but she was looking ahead to the next task, and one was soon jerked out of any sentimental repining."

Many of the women spoke regretfully of the end of Ruth Sayre's presidency, but she said, "A leader stays in office long enough to make her contribution but not long enough to keep others from making theirs." Her successor would be an Australian ranch woman, Mrs. Alice Berry.

According to Stella Bell, "The Royal York Hotel gave a very grand suite for the world president and the general secretary; the decorations were pseudo Chinese in a darkish green with dragons everywhere, and the plumbing in the bathroom was a little erratic. Kindly people kept sending us sheaves of long gladioli, and these we would lay out, like Ophelia, in one of the baths. As we rushed in from meetings to get ready hastily for some grand reception, the cry was, 'Which bath isn't full of flowers?' "

Ruth Sayre had no intention of retiring from the ACWW picture as Mrs. Watt had done. She took on the leadership of a survey committee to restructure the organization because, she said, "The attempts to 'neaten' the constitution had been done in piecemeal fashion. It was evident that there were gaps in the constitution, the procedure, and the administration."

The ACWW had returned to the land of its birth for the seventh Triennial, and Mrs. Sayre paid tribute to the Marchioness of Aberdeen and Temair, to Mrs. Alfred Watt, and to Mrs. Adelaide Hoodless, who started the Canadian Women's Institute. She said, "The idea remains the same—women getting together to do community housekeeping. ACWW has a vast, global network of small, active, voluntary groups of country women. They are dedicated to the idea of working together to improve life for the homes and families of their communities. The pattern of local programs built around this idea doesn't change appreciably from country to country. They attack the world's problems on their own doorstep, beginning where they are with what they have."

Speaking often during the ten-day conference, Mrs. Sayre said, "It is easy to do what is usual—to get into a rut. Please do not get into a rut. Have the courage to go ahead. Have a large vision, and the larger your vision, the more you will be able to do."

She talked of the importance of face-to-face contacts, saying, "They bring a personal knowledge of facts about other countries, dispel false and sentimental illusions, and help us to understand that there are differences in cultures which we have now, in our small world, to learn to live with."

The importance of women as creators of attitudes was another theme Ruth Sayre brought out in Toronto. She said, "Men may make the road, but it is the mothers who teach the children to walk upon it," and she noted, "In every country, no matter how subordinate the position of women in the life of the community, if changes in traditions and habits are to be made, they [women] must first see their value."

Mrs. Sayre had encouraged Louise Rosenfeld to attend the Toronto conference, and she pressed her into service there, asking her to schedule an American tour for women from Egypt, Pakistan, and India. Miss Rosenfeld recalls, "At a banquet in Toronto, a man preceded Mrs. Sayre and then introduced her. Ruth quipped, 'The cock croweth, but the hen delivereth the goods!' "

On August 21, near the end of the conference, the delegates voted down a motion that ACWW support the principle of equal pay for men and women proposed by a United Kingdom delegation. The arguments against it have become all too familiar and do not bear repeating, but some national delegations were split in their views.

Ruth Sayre, who had a good sense of when to push and when to withdraw, said, "This means, of course, that this vast body of women should work toward equal pay for both sexes. As we represent specifically rural women, the implications will be far-reaching, particularly in relation to life on the land."

In the end the delegates at least promised to work for women's suffrage wherever it had been denied. They also reaffirmed support of the UN, endorsed the principle of international commodity agreements to promote world trade, asked UNESCO to help reduce the world's illiteracy by providing more fundamental education for women, resolved to work for more research in the production and distribution of food and other goods, determined to be better informed on major legisla-

*Ruth Sayre was appointed to President
Eisenhower's new Agricultural Advisory
Committee, and Raymond Sayre was appointed
to the National Farm Credit Board in 1953,
prompting a farm editor to call them
"the most important single farm family
in the nation."*

tion, agreed to encourage more international exchange of rural youth, and urged that realistic technical assistance programs to under-developed countries be expanded.

As Ruth Sayre handed over to Alice Berry the responsibility of leading six million women, she had every confidence in the woman who said, "My heart and thoughts will always be with those on the land." There were others, too, young and eager women who were preparing themselves to carry on the work in years to come. The ACWW now truly was what she had so often called it, "a *voice* in international councils, a *movement* to improve the lot of country women, a *fellowship* to build the bridge of understanding and a window to the world.

She was quite willing to take the challenge she had given to the delegates, "Give me your life and I will make it a spade to dig the foundations of a new world, a crowbar to pry loose the rocks, a trowel to bind stone on stone and make a wall. You cannot build that wall alone, but you can make sure that you have put one stone in place and made it secure.''

With her own stone firmly in place, Ruth Sayre stepped down but certainly not out of ACWW. Invitations for the 1956 Triennial had been issued by Ceylon, Australia, and Scotland, and she intended to go wherever the conference was set.

The time in Mexico with Raymond was a holiday for Ruth. They enjoyed leisurely dinners, admired the murals of Diego Rivera and strolled in the plazas of Mexico City thinking how grand it was to be away together. They drove to Taxco, Cuernavaca, and Patzcuaro in a rented car and dined with Senor and Senora Juan Enrich, who had bought sheep from Raymond. All too soon it was time to go home.

At Ackworth Ruth found a telegram from Earl Warren, Chief Justice of the United States, asking her to accept an appointment to a commission on judicial and congressional salaries. She did so immediately, believing the honor to be one of the highest that had come to her.

Then Raymond Sayre took his turn in the limelight. His fifteen years of service as a director of the Omaha Federal Land Bank culminated in his appointment (confirmation pending) to the National Farm Credit Board.

J. S. Russell, farm editor of the *Des Moines Register,* wrote, ''This appointment probably makes the Sayre family the most important single farm family in the nation.''

Almost immediately there were rumors of another high government post for Mrs. Sayre. Her name, together with that of Mrs. Hiram Cole Houghton of Red Oak, was mentioned for the UN post, and the *Des Moines Register* wrote, ''Mrs. Sayre is reported to have a more general support and appears to be certain of receiving one of two jobs for which she is being considered.''

True D. Morse, under secretary of agriculture, put an end to the suspense with a phone call to Ackworth asking Ruth Sayre to be a member of the new Agricultural Advisory Committee being appointed by President Eisenhower.

With Raymond's confirmation still hanging fire, Mrs. Sayre said, ''Should we both be appointed? Some suggested that I step aside, but we both were appointed, and I went to Washington in September as the first and only woman on the advisory board. Our job was to help develop federal farm programs to best meet the needs of the entire farming population and the consumers.''

Together in the national capital, the Sayres saw their new jobs as the flowering of what Ruth called ''all our work together to help build a better life for country people.''

*Mrs. Sayre was the only woman on the Agricultural
Advisory Committee seen here on the White
House steps with the president and Secretary of
Agriculture Ezra Taft Benson.*

This rapid succession of developments occurred just a few weeks after the expiration of Ruth Sayre's ACWW presidency, and she shifted gears quickly. It was, as she said, "a period of adjustment in agriculture from war to changing technology. High support prices had piled up surpluses to glut the market when wartime demand had fallen off. The commission was to advise Ezra Taft Benson, and he could accept or reject our advice."

When she accepted the appointment, Ruth Sayre said, "My personal reaction is that government can't grant security to the farmer or anyone else, but it can help create conditions and the climate in which farmers can operate successfully in an industrialized economy."

She posed with the president, Secretary Benson, and the rest of the commission on the north portico of the White House smiling broadly, but she declined comment on the board's first meeting, according to one newspaper account, "possibly to prove to her male colleagues that a woman doesn't tell everything she knows."

Ruth Sayre did say, "There is no one solution to the complicated farm problem. If anybody knew a good or pat answer, it would have been given long ago."

Secretary Benson opened each session with prayer, and Mrs. Sayre noted wryly, "I didn't always feel that what was done was accomplished with Divine guidance. We talked about price support, utilization of excess reserves, and farm employment. Recommendations were to be confidential, but I was amazed to find them in the *Des Moines Register* when I got home."

In addition to her new duties, Ruth Sayre was reappointed as a member of the U.S. national commission for UNESCO, the only woman to serve with Stanley Ruttenberg, CIO director of Education and Research; Luther Evans, Library of Congress; Senator Charles Tobey of New Hampshire; Elvin Stakeman, former president of the American Association for the Advancement of Science; Judge Homer S. Brown, former member of the Pennsylvania House of Representatives; and Walter H. C. Laves, chairman of the U.S. national commission for UNESCO and former deputy general of that body.

In early October Eleanor Roosevelt was scheduled to confer with officials of the Iowa Association for the UN and speak during Human Rights Week at the University Church of Christ, Des Moines. Trustees of the church refused to allow Mrs. Roosevelt to speak there, and Mrs. Sayre, who was to introduce the former First Lady, waited in chagrin while negotiations were made to move the meeting to the KRNT Theater. Church objections ranged from a belief that the meeting would be "a lot of politics" to the impression that Mrs. Roosevelt had "brought back liquor from abroad."

Early in November there was more talk of Ruth Sayre becoming a candidate for the United States Senate. The *Indianola Record-Herald* wrote, "This paper suggested Mrs. Sayre in 1948 and has no reason to retract one thought of what was said at that time. She is the one candidate of whom we can think who would, more than any other, leave Senator Guy Gillette well in second place for reelection."

The newspaper conceded that running for office would be a sacrifice, adding, "Now, if anybody can persuade Mrs. Sayre to make the sacrifice and show Mr. Sayre how he can spend part of his time in Washington with her, the *Record-Herald* is ready to take off its coat and go to work."

Again Raymond said, "'I don't believe you'd better do that," and again Ruth decided that she didn't want to do it.

Writing in the *Des Moines Register*, Elizabeth Clarkson Zwart told how Roger Fleming had greeted the Sayres' son Bill in a Des Moines hotel lobby, asking, "Where's your mother?" Bill's answer was, "I don't know."

The peripatetic Ruth Sayre moved far and fast, but still it was an exaggeration when another reporter wrote that she said, "I'd forgotten that I have to speak in Washington tonight. You'll have to feed the chickens."

The year was turning fast, and after the annual convention of the AFBF, Mrs. Sayre would take time out for a family Christmas and some long talks with John about the experiences of his first semester at Simpson College.

18

The Valley of the Shadow

IN mid-January 1954 the Commission on Judicial and Congressional Salaries proposed the first pay raise in those categories since 1946, and with that job accomplished, Ruth Sayre was ready for new endeavors.

In February she spoke at the Montana Farm Institute and the annual Farm and Home convention at the University of Kentucky, sharing her expertise on technical assistance.

"People fear change from what they understand to something new and unknown," she said. "They ask only to live out their lives unmolested. We are in danger of stifling the initiative of the people with too much money and too much dependence on American aid. We are leading the people of the underdeveloped countries to expect too much too soon. We must be careful about the people we send to these countries. They must be missionaries in the best sense of the word—not people tired of their jobs in the United States who want a free junket. They must be willing to live under difficult conditions and be patient, humble, not sentimental, and not too aggressive."

She also challenged her audiences by saying, "No matter where I have traveled, I have been struck by the ability of women in many other lands to find rich resources for happiness and enjoyment within themselves and within the environment in which they are. The life on a farm in Kenya is about as far from the beaten path as one can imagine. The roads are so bad they are simply endured. The mail comes two or three times a week, the telephone service is something less than reliable, there is no television and not too much good reception on radio, but I found shelves and shelves of well-read books, both old and new, and

At a 1954 White House Conference on Highway Safety in Washington, Mrs. Sayre presented a safe-driving citation to Pat Nixon, the young wife of Vice-President Richard M. Nixon.

people who knew about and had a keen interest in world affairs because they had made the most of what their environment could give them—time to read and do.''

At a three-day White House Conference on Highway Safety in mid-February, Ruth Sayre presented a scroll recognizing twenty-four years of accident-free driving to Pat Nixon, the young wife of the vice-president.

Women at the conference were entertained at a reception at the Sheraton-Carlton Hotel, and the *Washington Times-Herald* reported, ''Mrs. Raymond Sayre, the good-looking chairman of the council, stood with the other council members to receive the guests at the entrance to the Carlton room. She looked very smart in a cocktail length black lace dress, and of course an orchid corsage.'' Ruth Sayre did not have, as Dorothy Houghton of Red Oak is said to have claimed, ''a two-orchid bosom,'' but she could manage one orchid very nicely.

Safety would be a basic concern with Ruth Sayre for the next seven years. She saw her job as "convincing people that accidents are preventable on the job, on the road, at play, and at home," and she began to organize safety seminars.

She said, "Women believe they should approach the problem of traffic safety primarily from the standpoint of individual responsibility. It is not possible to rely alone on the three Es—engineering, enforcement, and education. We should also rely on the three As of individual responsibility: awareness of what I need to do, acceptance of what I ought to do, and action for what I will do."

Her appeal to women was direct and personal, "Women, you have most at stake in this business of preserving life on the highways. Injuries to yourselves, to your husbands, to your children can mean for you untold tragedy in terms of physical pain, financial loss, the disruption of all the stability that you can strive for in your homes."

Later, she noted, "Everyone was for safety, but there were no new approaches. They asked the women's conference board of the National Safety Council to suggest a theme, and I said the council should do more than quote accident statistics. It should have its own special projects, and I suggested a defensive driving course for moving about in modern-day traffic. The idea caught on, and I took the course myself."

Now that she no longer was president of the Associated Women of the AFBF, Ruth Sayre felt free to participate in partisan politics, and she attended the Republican Women's Centennial Conference at the Statler in Washington in early April.

In Chicago Ruth Sayre worked with four other judges to choose the Most Successful Homemaker of 1954. The criteria were, "In what way has she been a pillar of spiritual and moral strength in her own home? In what way has she done an exceptional job of managing her family income? Is she known as a good cook—if so, why? In what way has she done her part in civic and church efforts? How does she, regardless of family income, maintain her personal and family appearance? Has she demonstrated her abilities in creating an appealing family home?"

Later, Ruth Sayre also helped judge entries in the American Farm Bureau Federation's National Dairy Sales Promotion contest.

May 5 was a fine day with the fragrance of blossoming fruit trees in the air. It was the second birthday of Ann, the daughter of Bill and Ruthann, and Mrs. Sayre had business in Des Moines but hoped to be back in time to share the birthday cake.

"Do you want me to drive you in?" Raymond asked.

"Don't bother, I can make it all right." Ruth told him, "You'd better be at Bill's place when the man comes to cut down the tree."

The tree to be felled was in the pasture north of Bill's house, where Ruthann and the excited children were getting ready for the birthday party, and no one had any idea that the celebration would be forgotten on that day.

The next time Ruth saw Raymond, he was in a hospital bed at Des Moines Lutheran with a broken leg. He grinned weakly and said, "The man yelled that the tree was falling, and I turned the wrong way and got caught in some bushes."

Ruth gave him a kiss and said with mock severity, "That's a fine thing for the husband of someone on the Safety Council to do!"

John drove his mother to Des Moines for the daily hospital visits, and when it seemed that Raymond could come home soon, they spoke of moving a bed downstairs for him. They were still discussing this as they came into the house and heard the phone ringing.

While they were driving back to Ackworth from Des Moines, Raymond Sayre had died of a blood clot. He had looked fine when they left him—it couldn't be! But it was. Raymond Sayre was dead at 61, gone before they could do all the things they had planned together. The date was May 24, 1954.

Sympathy poured in from all over the world. From British East Africa, Marjorie Patersen wrote, "I have often thought of what a wonderfully considerate and understanding husband you must have, as you told me he was an enthusiastic supporter of all your good works and in his own right contributed so greatly to the welfare of the farming communities in the United States."

It would be five years before Ruth Sayre could come to terms with her loss enough to talk about it in a *Farm Journal* article told to Gertrude Dieken, but when she did, it would be with the hope of helping others cope with what *Wallaces' Farmer* called "the overpowering loneliness that creeps in on Sunday afternoons and twilights."

Again she would speak to the condition of so many, saying, "Suddenly part of your world is gone. It is a drastic severance, as if you had lost a part of your own self—an arm or a leg. Now you must literally learn to walk again—alone."

Raymond's death was a crisis of faith for Ruth Sayre, and she came through it seeing death as part of life. "It would be good if we were more at home with this idea throughout our lives, not morbidly but realistically. Instead of 'everything dies,' it might help us to think of it as 'everything changes.'"

"Widows should not 'carry on as we always did,'" she advised, "nothing will ever be the same again. Build a new life. Take time to make decisions about the future. At first, it's easy to say, 'Why bother to paint the living room or get a new screen door? I am just here alone.' But you have to keep home attractive for children and friends.''

She mentioned how much she depended on Raymond for ideas and for bolstering her own ideas and said, ''I couldn't face going into town for groceries, which we had always done together. I couldn't go back to that hospital with its wracking memories.

''I felt the world was inhabited only by couples. You will be left out. The routine of a job would have been a godsend to me. The easiest way is to lean on your children. I have tried hard not to do that. My son Bill dropped in after chores on those beautiful but painfully lonely Sunday afternoons and said, 'Better come by for supper.'

''I took up needlepoint, which I never did before—the same with quilt piecing from family attics. I had a binge of cleaning and throwing away, but I kept things of interest to make a scrapbook for the children.''

Raymond's death came just as the heavy travel for ACWW had ended, and Ruth had hoped to spend more time at home or traveling with her husband.

''Suddenly I wasn't needed anymore, it seemed.'' she said, but Raymond's accident gave her an even stronger reason for working hard on safety projects. She said, ''It took on a new meaning.''

Always a realist, she said, ''I have no pat advice. The death of a husband leaves a woman peculiarly broken.'' The advice she did offer consisted of ''being a person all your life, not just a wife. Have some interests of your own. Cultivate a sort of aloneness. A young woman should prepare for widowhood when she gets married. Learn to make decisions and go ahead on your own even if you are married. Some women stop driving when they get a husband, not a symptom of dependence, but probably laziness.''

The practicalities were, she said, ''talking about the business side, discussing wills, insurance, joint bank accounts. You must understand family business. When a woman loses her husband, she has to make important decisions about business matters, and that seems to be just the last straw. You couldn't care less just when you need to care most.''

She rejected the words, '' 'Til death do us part,'' saying, ''No, for my husband's spirit lives in the fields he tended, the trees he planted— in our children and grandchildren and in our faith that we are *not* left alone.''

Being a farm woman helped Ruth Sayre bear the greatest tragedy of her life. She said, ''I have lived for so many years with the laws of nature's seasons that I believe it was a little easier for me to accept this. . . . We farm women know everything 'dies,' '' but rather than thinking of death as an ending, she said, ''actually the spirit of a person lives on with us and contributes to our lives after death. Just as a plant plowed under nurtures new plants that nurture new plants—and so on.''

In the writing of ''Left Alone,'' Gertrude Dieken captured the essence of Mrs. Sayre's thought and expression perfectly, working with the keen sensitivity gained from long association and friendship.

Bill Sayre became his mother's farming partner, and Ruth Sayre tried to collect the broken strands of her existence. Outwardly, she was serene and pleasant, but inwardly, she was devastated.

Mrs. C. C. Inman, writing in the *Farm Bureau Spokesman* for June 19, 1954, said, ''I think of the calmness of her face at Raymond's memorial service even though we know her heart was torn. As she passed some of her friends and fellow workers, she saluted us with raised gloved hand as if to say, 'I am glad you are with me.' ''

At the thirty-sixth annual convention of the AFBF in New York City, Ruth Sayre received the distinguished service award of the federation ''for outstanding contributions to the progress of agriculture'' from Allan Kline, who was accorded the same honor.

Even more gratifying to Mrs. Sayre was the formal adoption of the Associated Women as part of the American Farm Bureau Federation after three years of discussion. She said, ''In Iowa, as in other states, women had always been partners. They didn't have to get in—they had always been in.''

Allan Kline said, ''I never cease to have the utmost respect for the ability of our farm women. I always believed we were missing an opportunity by not encouraging them to work in the whole program along with their husbands—really being a part of the organization. We finally got it accomplished in 1954 with the efforts of Mrs. Raymond Sayre and other women like her in the states. Often they act ahead of the menfolk, and we don't always like that, but God bless them. We need the girls!''

19

Sorrows and Strengths

RETURNING from a trip to Mexico in late February 1955, Ruth Sayre found Raymond's mother seriously ill and canceled most of her appointments to spend time with the sweet-faced Mamie Sayre.

When she left her mother-in-law's bedside briefly on March 19 to attend the seventeenth annual National Farm Institute, the "Country Air" column in *Wallaces' Farmer* commented: "Mrs. Sayre—great lady of the whole show—she speaks to the point—keeps still at the period and has done some thinking before she tackles either. . . . It took tremendous poise to stand at the speakers' table while the audience rose in silent memorial to her late husband, Raymond Sayre."

Thus reminded of her deepest grief, Ruth Sayre endured more sadness when Mamie Sayre died March 24, but she had work to do, and while she was in Washington for a meeting of the Agricultural Advisory Commission, she received a citation at the national 4-H camp.

Mrs. Sayre was asked to serve on a Social Responsibility advisory group for the National Council of Churches, and she shouldered that responsibility with her usual willingness until she read a manuscript in preparation for publication which the group seemed to approve. She did not approve because the writer's criticism of food producers in their relation to the hungry of the world struck at the Farm Bureau, in her opinion.

She resigned from the advisory group, explaining, "I do not feel that I can be at all objective about the subject. . . . I am surely one of the ones about whom the study is written. I cannot and would not want to disassociate myself from the Farm Bureau and my own responsibility for whatever it has done, and therefore I feel I should not be considered a member of the advisory group.

"The friends and colleagues with whom I have worked over the years would wonder, I am sure, why I had identified myself with a study which tends to pass judgment on them from an ethical viewpoint. I am too much a Methodist to believe that others can interpret the Bible for me, and I have for too long been a part of the Farm Bureau to pass ethical judgments on others for Farm Bureau policies for which I am also responsible. In order that there will be no feeling that I have an obligation to the National Council, I have paid my own expenses for the meeting."

Ruth Sayre's ethics were anything but situational; she knew without question where her loyalties lay.

Although her pace had slackened somewhat, Mrs. Sayre flew to London to meet with the ACWW Survey Committee and participated in a Traffic Institute and seminar on safe driving at Northwestern University, Evanston, Illinois.

On August 22, a third child, Mary Alice, was born to Bill and Ruthann Sayre, and Ruth Sayre was a delighted grandmother for the fifth time.

Severance of the ties between the Extension Service and the Farm Bureau in 1955 saddened Ruth Sayre. It seemed almost like the divorce of two good friends. The separation was triggered by an edict from Ezra Taft Benson to the effect that Extension could no longer accept funds from private organizations or submit to the direction of such organizations in the conduct of its responsibilities.

The Iowa Farm Bureau was distressed by Benson's directive, but, fearing the loss of federal funds, accepted it. Farm Bureau members realized that though the fruits of the Extension–Farm Bureau marriage could be defended, the morality of the relationship between a government agency and a private farm organization could not.

Mrs. Sayre had made arrangements to lead a delegation of farm women on a tour of the Middle East, and as she prepared for the trip, her family was concerned that tensions in that area would erupt into actual fighting, and the American women would be caught in the middle of it. However, Ruth Sayre was not to be deflected from her plans.

Arriving in Cairo, she saw soldiers with a big machine gun in a city square trying to recruit young Egyptians for the army, but, in spite of Arab bitterness toward Israel, "most people seemed to be going on as usual."

Mrs. Sayre reported that the problems were poverty, ignorance, disease, and lack of water, but "the people are thinking mostly about the 'injustice' forced upon the Arabs whose land became the new Israel.''

Water scarcity meant that no grass could grow in the villages, and Ruth Sayre sympathized with the housewife who "must always contend with dust. Her small house is made of mud and straw bricks with a dirt floor and no windows.''

She also sympathized with the fellahin who worked hard to raise enough food and cotton on a half acre of land, earning thirty cents a day if they worked for a landlord. Their families seldom saw meat or milk.

"The amount of hand labor here is beyond belief,'' she wrote, "for instance, workers are excavating for Cairo's new Hilton Hotel with picks and are carrying the dirt out in bushel baskets. Men are not slaves like those the Pharaohs used to build the Pyramids, but they are not working any differently.''

She did see some hope in the situation through government promotion of agricultural research, land reform, and irrigation, but she noted, "Any Extension Service work for women is still only on paper.''

Mrs. Matilda Greiss, who had attended the Toronto Triennial, entertained the American women royally in her Cairo home and told them about the Egyptian Women's League for Rural Development, which was starting a demonstration farm. At first, the Egyptian women were afraid to come to the farm, and those who dared to come were veiled. Eventually, however, they came eagerly, and Mrs. Sayre and her party found them willing subjects for photographs.

In Iraq Ruth Sayre gazed at the ruins of Babylon, the banquet hall of Belshazzar, and the den where Daniel was thrown to the lions. She had no difficulty imagining Abraham traveling with his flocks in Mesopotamia, for people tended their flocks in the same manner now, plowing with a wooden stick and living in tents.

She was told of the disastrous floods of the Tigris and Euphrates and could see the condition of the worn-out soil for herself. In this most poverty-stricken country of the Middle East, she said, "Living in Iraq seems to be a matter of making up your mind to accept dust and dirt and very little water,'' and she could see that tribal feuding and an attitude of "every man for himself'' militated against progress.

Bertha Strange, a home economist from Texas, welcomed the American party to the little oasis of hope in the sand where she was offering technical assistance of the best kind. Ruth Sayre said of her, "Bertha Strange is the epitome of a modern-day missionary, the kind of person you wish the United States had in all our overseas projects. She is willing to live in the village, drinking yogurt with the people in their own mud huts, picking up crying babies, and loving the school children who come to her with their sore eyes, uncombed hair, and ragged clothes.

"She has taught some of the people to grow fresh vegetables in spite of the dry, hot days and misgivings of many. She has helped establish a school where even girls (often neglected in the Middle East) are welcome. At school they have milk; vitamin tablets from UNICEF, the United Nations agency for helping children; and bread they have brought from home. . . . To teach children who have never sat at a table or used forks or spoons to eat strange foods in a new way is an accomplishment hard to imagine back home."

In Iran Ruth Sayre concluded, "One thing I have learned on this trip—you can't lump all the countries of the Middle East together. Each has problems and characteristics all its own. For instance, Iran, though it is Moslem, is not an Arab state. The people are not Arabs but Iranians. They speak their own language and have their own proud history."

She observed the building boom in Teheran and the sharp contrast of poverty in the country. Loath to leave Iran, the cradle of agriculture, Ruth Sayre reflected, "With all we know now, Iran can be made to bloom again."

Looking upon the visit to Israel and Jordan as a pilgrimage to the Holy Land, Mrs. Sayre eagerly anticipated seeing Bethlehem, Nazareth, and the Garden of Gethsemane, but when she arrived, she knew that the present was crowding out the past. The barbed wire and passport check at the Mandelbaum Gate by the Jordanians was followed by an Israeli check.

"We need to know what is happening here," she told one of her traveling companions, "for there will be no peace until the issues of the Middle East are given more consideration by the rest of the world."

Americans were supposed to be neutral in the Arab-Israeli situation, but, Mrs. Sayre said, "As far as I can tell, nobody is. Both Israelis and Jordanians propagandized us liberally with their sides of the story, and both have something to be said for them. But the sad part is that so much bitterness now exists, a compromise is hard to find."

The women visited the Arab refugee camps, where the homeless people lived in tents and were fed for about eight cents a day per person, and Ruth Sayre said, "A most serious circumstance is that half the Arab refugees are children fifteen years or under who have been growing up without education or anything to do."

Driving through the hills of Moab, Mrs. Sayre could imagine Ruth, her namesake, watching the sheep graze along rocky creeks fringed with pink oleanders. Near Mount Nebo, where Moses first saw the Promised

*A 1956 Food and Agriculture Organization
meeting in Tokyo gave Ruth Sayre the chance to
recruit ACWW members over the teacups.*

Land, she observed, "It no longer looked like a promised land—so bare, so brown, so rocky."

From the Dead Sea, the women took a side trip, driving five miles over a winding track of sand and stones to see the caves where the Dead Sea Scrolls were found.

In Amman, Jordan, they were happy to meet Miss Dejani, the first Home Economics Extension director they had found in the Middle East, and she told them that thirty-four women's organizations flourished in Jordan.

The long, black cotton gown decorated with red and yellow cross-stitching which Ruth Sayre bought in Bethlehem was one example of the village costumes the women wore, but across the border in Israel, the charming, traditional dress disappeared. The people looked contemporary and western.

Mrs. Sayre understood the Israeli problem of making farmers of people from so many diverse skills and backgrounds and found that "getting back to the land" was more a matter of ideology than of economics.

"I was disappointed in the holy places at Bethlehem and Nazareth," she said, "the places Christ was supposed to have visited were covered with mosques. Only the Sea of Galilee seemed the same. I got up early one morning to walk down the rocky shore and watch the sun come up over the ancient hills. And to lift a small prayer that somehow He would help us as a nation do our part in bringing peace again to this land of great trouble.''

One of the problems of the trip was eating, and Mrs. Sayre said, ''I was a guest in a house where the woman said she had washed the beans in detergent and disinfectant.''

Laura Lane, who served as Mrs. Sayre's editor for the series of articles on the Middle East trip that ran in the *Farm Journal* beginning in January 1956, said, ''Mrs. Sayre had an unusual grasp of the situation and of the conflict which had only begun then and would continue for several decades and who knows how much longer?

''She then spoke of the area as the Holy Land. She could see both sides of the confrontation and recognized weaknesses in each position. I think she was the first person I ever knew personally who didn't take a romanticized view of Israel simply because it was the Holy Land. She recognized that some of the dispossessed Arabs had a few points on their side: a long history of possession, history, even fairness.

Mrs. Sayre made new friends in the Philippines during a 1956 meeting of the Women's Rural Improvement Clubs of the World.

"As I recall, some of our readers looked on the conflict in the light of biblical prophecy alone. They felt that Mrs. Sayre was pro-Arab. An extremely small minority wrote in to that effect. I felt her analytical view of the situation after talking with many people from all strata of life did much to inform our readers about the true state of affairs in the Middle East.

"As a reporter, I valued my connections with Mrs. Sayre for many reasons: She was always a good friend, but she was patient with questions, and she was always very good at explaining the why of her position."

In early May 1956 Ruth Sayre attended a Traffic Safety meeting in Atlantic City, and later that month she accepted a position on the National Advisory Committee for Citizens for Eisenhower. She could not attend the Citizens for Ike meeting in Washington May 30 and June 1 because her presence was required at a regional White House Traffic Safety conference in San Francisco on those dates.

She proved her worth to the Eisenhower campaign by devising an effective question and answer radio format. Question: "What do you think President Eisenhower has done to move the country toward peace and to reduce international tensions?" Answer: (by a typical farm wife) "The president stands for peace and has made the United States stand for peace in the eyes of the people of the world. The president has guided the country through many difficult international situations without involving us in war. The president has brought about the cessation of fighting in Korea." When Ruth Sayre felt free to campaign, she went at it with all her might.

In the summer of 1956 Helen showed symptoms that plunged the entire family into deep dread. On August 31 she entered the Framingham hospital for the removal of some lymph glands, and the word "melanoma," so musical in its pronunication and so terrible in its meaning, reentered Ruth Sayre's vocabulary. After a week with Helen in mid-September, Mrs. Sayre flew to Washington for a succession of meetings, then returned to Framingham to stay as long as possible before going home to pack for a lengthy overseas trip.

In October Ruth Sayre flew to Tokyo for a Food and Agriculture Organization meeting. She also would attend a home economics meeting there and visit Japan International Christian University. Kneeling on tatami mats to drink tea with kimono-clad women she tucked in a bit of missionary work for ACWW.

A visit with Mrs. Hacherio Yuasa, a 1922 Simpson College graduate, was wedged into a busy schedule of sight-seeing, flower arranging demonstrations, and a Kabuki dance performance.

Attending a meeting of the Women's Rural Improvement Clubs of the World in the Philippines, she met Ramon Magsaysay, who gave her a picture of himself inscribed, "To our friend Mrs. Raymond Sayre with highest esteem." She spent ten days in the Philippines studying United States technical assistance programs in agriculture and home economics.

A visit to Corregidor brought back memories of World War II, Dick Jacobs, and Helen's grief on the summer day when she learned that her young husband was missing in action. It seemed all wrong that Helen should suffer both then and now.

After learning the results of the United States national election in Manilla, Mrs. Sayre went on to Thailand and Burma for more inspection and study, then enjoyed a reunion with Indian friends in Calcutta, Madras, and Bombay.

She had planned to climax this trip with the ACWW Triennial in Ceylon, but the Suez Canal crisis brought about the postponement of the conference, and instead she flew to Zurich and Geneva, then to London for Christmas with Alice. On the way home, she would spend several weeks with Helen, whose health was now a matter of grave concern.

20

Going On

IN the years between ACWW Triennials, Ruth Sayre was unrelentingly busy with the work of the Survey Committee.

Stella Bell says, "It was mostly carried out by mail, but with one hectic week spent in the Garden Hotel, Cambridge, England—the only hot week that summer. We worked with the French windows open and the curtains drawn to keep the sun out. Mrs. Sayre was indefatigable, and everyone worked from early morning to quite late in the evening, but without her drive, the enormous amount of ground could not have been covered.

"This was a difficult period in ACWW, for we had a number of wonderful women all wanting the same result—the best possible for ACWW—but seeing different ways of achieving their aims. Looking back, one also realizes that there were misunderstandings because those of us who think we speak the same language very often mean quite different things by the same words and phrases. Mrs. Sayre, I am sure, realized that many of the things she felt essential would upset some of the people who had given most to ACWW in the early difficult days, but if she thought a thing right for the organization, then she was prepared to go ahead and fight for it."

In the early months of 1957, Ruth Sayre's date book was uncharacteristically blank because she was spending so much time with Helen in Massachusetts. She took her daughter to some of the best cancer specialists in the nation.

When Helen seemed to be holding her own, Mrs. Sayre came home, and now, as John Sayre puts it, "Mother's pace was different, and she could do some of the Ackworth and Indianola activities she enjoyed."

She joined the Business and Professional Women; attended meetings of her PEO chapter, the Pi Phi Alumnae Club, and the Thimble Club; and explored new interests as a member of the planning commission for the Des Moines Art Center. Her definition of art was "The doing in the very best way of the thing that needs to be done."

A farm meeting took her to Oklahoma in May, she attended a polio meeting in New York later that month, and June 23 she met with Mrs. Sewell at the Farm Bureau Women's Conference in Des Moines, leaving for Ceylon via England the next day.

Always interested in developing the leadership potential in younger women, Ruth Sayre had met with Alice Van Wert from Hampton, Iowa, offering expert briefing for the Triennial in Ceylon.

Mrs. Van Wert, who became a young widow the same year Raymond Sayre died, says, "I was highly privileged to have Mrs. Sayre's help in preparing me to be a participating delegate at this conference. In Ceylon I could see the results of her in-depth study and research of other international organizations as she sought the best type of structure for ACWW. She carried with her all the correspondence which reflected the majority agreement of all her committee. However, it was a great disappointment to her and others to see some of those same people, influenced by the old dictatorial leadership, express a different viewpoint in very lively discussions at the conference."

The report suggested a three-tier organization consisting of the conference, the council including the officers of ACWW and representatives from all societies meeting once a year between conferences, and a small executive or general purpose committee. The six elected members no longer were included, and proxies were eliminated.

Mrs. Sayre later wrote, "The report created much division of opinion between those who wanted to keep the status quo—the old executive committee setup—and those who felt that the time had come to make the administration more international and more representative of the societies. Many of the American members, particularly, felt that they were disenfranchised. They had by this time the largest number of member societies of any country in ACWW and were supplying some seventy percent of the ACWW budget. It was impossible for them to send representatives to London for four or six meetings a year. And in spite of all efforts, it was impossible to find proxies in London who had any knowledge of the organization and program of United States societies."

Mrs. Van Wert reported that "the air was electrified" by the clash of opinions. "There were those who were adamant about ruling all from the London office and letting the president be more or less of a figurehead. According to them, her responsibility was not to be involved in the business or the office, but to be a speaker and travel about representing the organization.''

Because of the postponement of the conference, attendance was low, and the heated discussion ended with acceptance of the Survey Report and deferment of action on it until the next Triennial, to be held in Edinburgh in 1959. In other words, the women tore the document apart and tabled it.

In spite of her deep disappointment in this reception of three years of hard work, Ruth Sayre remained affable and interested in the other business of the conference.

Gerda Van Beekhoff of the Netherlands writes, ''I am still convinced that, if Ruth hadn't been with me in Ceylon in 1957, I really never would have stood for election in 1959. My life would have been so much the poorer. Had Mrs. Sayre not been in Ceylon, I never would have dared to accept the nomination as ACWW's next president.''

Prior to the conference, Mrs. Sayre had attended a seminar for women students of Southeast Asia who had heard of ACWW but were not familiar with its workings, goals, and aims. The seminar was held in Kandy, the city of Ceylon's ancient kings.

Mrs. Van Beekhoff says, ''I had heard Mrs. Sayre speak in Amsterdam, Copenhagen, and Toronto, but I was an admirer from a distance. When we finally met eye to eye, it just clicked, and I knew I had found a friend forever.''

At Kandy, Mrs. Van Beekhoff was approached by a delegate from Rhodesia, Mrs. Nora Price, concerning her willingness to stand for president. The two women had met on a bus trip through the northeastern United States following the Toronto conference. As they sat together on the bus and speculated about who the next president would be, Mrs. Van Beekhoff says, ''I never thought it might be me.

''When we went back to the hotel, I fled to Mrs. Sayre's room to tell her of my confusion and get her opinion. When I stopped talking, Mrs. Sayre with that special twinkle in her eyes said, 'Of course you'll be able to do it! Why shouldn't you stand? You are young, and we are badly in need of younger persons in office in ACWW. Once again— why shouldn't you? Explain to your husband what it's all about, and I'm sure he'll be proud of you!' I've never forgotten that moment: Mrs. Sayre as a rock of strength smiling and just saying, 'Why shouldn't you?'

''All through the years of my presidency, I knew I could count on Ruth—always there was the right word at the right moment, the little pat on the back one is needing from time to time. Her delightful twinkle and little nod of approval always gave me a very warm feeling of friendship for this remarkably gifted woman.

"I never met anybody else who could put a certain complicated situation in a nutshell so that it became clear to everybody, though at first it had seemed incomprehensible. No other person could have brought the findings of the Survey Committee so down-to-earth as did Mrs. Sayre. As Ruth put it, 'ACWW has outgrown its clothes and is in need of a new dress.' Just as simple as all that. It made explaining to our members so very much easier. Everybody suddenly understood."

That instantaneous understanding did not occur in Ceylon, however, and Ruth Sayre's patience was sorely tried.

She returned home in August in time for a safety seminar in Evanston, Illinois, on the nineteenth of the month, and then George Coolidge phoned with the chilling news that Helen was hospitalized in Framingham.

Mrs. Sayre flew to Massachusetts immediately, and Helen's condition soon warranted a transfer to Boston City Hospital. No hope was offered, but Helen was brave, and when she was granted the mercy of sleep, her mother sat beside her and anguished, convinced that things would have been different had the lymph glands been removed earlier.

On Sunday, September 8, 1957, Helen Sayre Jacobs Coolidge died at Boston City Hospital, and Ruth Sayre was with her to the last. Family members who gathered for the funeral included Martha Scott, Bill Buxton, and Bill and John Sayre. Services were held at the Plymouth Congregational church in Framingham at 2 p.m. on Tuesday, September 10, with burial in Edgell Grove Cemetery.

Mrs. Sayre stayed in Framingham for the rest of the month, controlling her own grief to make things easier for her son-in-law, nine-year-old Ruggie, and Cindy, who was seven. Martha Scott also stayed for a time to support her sister and her niece's family.

Helen had been active in her church, the Woman's Club, Girl Scouts, Cub Scouts, PTA, and the hospital volunteers as long as her health allowed, and she was greatly missed in the community as well as by her family.

Losing her firstborn while she still struggled with the pain of Raymond's death was a heavy blow to Ruth Sayre. In her date books of the coming years, she always marked their January birthdays as times for special memories. Now, she summoned her reserves of strength and went on.

In early October she attended a safety seminar in Knoxville, Tennessee, and in November she entertained Mrs. Evelyn Amarteifio, general secretary of the Federation of Ghana Women, who was touring the United States on a State Department program. Mrs. Amarteifio wore a brightly printed native dress called a ''mamma'' for the elegant dinner for eighteen hosted in her honor by Ruth and John Sayre at Ackworth.

''I always invited visitors from other countries to stay with us,'' Mrs. Sayre said, and she had some words of advice for others planning to entertain foreign guests: ''Read about the guest's country in advance, and first of all, learn to pronounce your guest's name. Even if you get it wrong, the effort is always appreciated. You should be able to ask intelligent questions about the country and encourage the guest to talk about home and family life.''

When the African guest departed, Ruth Sayre went to the Iowa Farm Bureau convention in Des Moines, and in early December she was in Washington, D.C., on Safety Council business. She was as comfortable chatting with William Randolph Hearst of the President's Committee for Traffic Safety as she was when passing the time of day with an Ackworth neighbor.

This year would see the end of Mrs. Sayre's service on the United States Department of Agriculture Advisory Committee on Foreign Agriculture, Trade and Technical Assistance, but she had added the President's Committee on Youth Fitness to her responsibilities and was listed among the 131 women appointed to high positions in the Eisenhower administration.

The Christmas mail brought many greetings from the Orient, and a woman from Lucknow, India, wrote, ''When I went to Calcutta after Ceylon and to the Southeast Asian Seminar, it was your inspiration and faith that provided me the strength to participate. With condolences for your daughter's death.''

Hard as she tried, Ruth Sayre could not keep busy enough to forget that Helen was gone. Solace could be found in the family that remained to her and in the easy company of the Older Youth Group, friends from high school and college who ''met whenever they felt like it,'' but wrapping Christmas presents for George, Ruggie, and Cindy brought a fresh stab of pain.

21

Some Time for Ruth

RUTH SAYRE always had started a new year with a burst of hard work, but the beginning of 1958 was more leisurely. She saw two movies in one week—a Disney picture with Bill's family and *Around the World in 80 Days* with John—and she also attended a lecture on Oriental art.

She soon got down to business, however with a mid-January meeting on ACWW resolutions in Chicago, a bank meeting at home, work on her income tax returns, and planning for a trip to London near the end of the month with her sister Martha. This would be Martha Scott's first trip abroad, and Ruth looked forward to being her cicerone.

On January 23, John was inducted into the army in Des Moines, and when Mrs. Sayre saw him off for Fort Leonard Wood the next day, she reflected how much easier it was to give up her younger son to the peacetime army than it had been to relinquish Bill to the marines at the height of World War II hostilities. Then she flew to Chicago to collect Martha for the overseas flight.

After three weeks of hard work in the ACWW office in London, Mrs. Sayre was free to enjoy being a tourist with Martha. The sisters visited Cornwall, Devon, Bath, Plymouth, and Exeter. They shopped for antiques and saw *The Mousetrap* and other plays in London's West End theaters. After a short side trip to Rome and Zurich with Alice, they resumed their happy rambling in England, visiting Stratford-on-Avon and Warwick Castle.

Frustrated in her search for more information on the English Buxtons, Mrs. Sayre commissioned a professional genealogy, and in the town of Buxton she bought a beautiful decanter in the form of a duck.

Meetings in Atlantic City and Washington preceded her return to Ackworth in March. In early April she attended safety meetings in Chicago and San Francisco, and she spent three days in Miami in late May.

John was be be sent to Munich, Germany, and he and his fiancee, Barbara Worth, whom he had met at Simpson, decided to marry before he left so she could join him in Germany. The wedding was to be held in the Methodist church at Monroe, Iowa, June 8, and as Ruth Sayre entertained an Egyptian guest a few days before the ceremony, she reflected that she never had arranged a full-scale wedding that required months of planning. Helen had taken all that responsibility on her own, and Alice never married. At any rate, she was experienced at being the mother of the bridegroom.

The day after the wedding, Mrs. Sayre was off to New York for a Country Women's Council meeting. On June 14 she attended the Iowa State College Centennial festivities in Ames, receiving an award "for making a unique contribution to the stature of Iowa State College." The following day she flew to New York for meetings of the National Foundation for Infantile Paralysis.

Her crowded schedule seemed back to normal with the Farm Bureau Summer Conference, planning meetings for an Art Center exhibit in the small town of Adel, a polio meeting in Des Moines, and a Health and Safety workshop in Seattle.

One of the happiest events of the summer was the July 15 birth of Elizabeth Ruth, the fourth child of Bill and Ruthann Sayre.

Between trips to Washington, New York, Toronto, Wichita, Topeka, and Kansas City in the fall, Mrs. Sayre found time for meetings of the Garden Club and the Thimble Club, and she was gratified by the success of the Dallas County art show at Adel, a pilot program for taking the resources of the Des Moines Art Center out to the people.

After attending the AFBF convention in Boston early in December, Ruth Sayre wrapped the Christmas presents she had purchased abroad: gloves for Cindy and Ann, puzzles for Ruggie and Billy, a blouse for Alice, and a doll for Mary. The gifts brought back happy memories of Rome, Lucerne, and England and of a holiday in which she had both time and money to spend.

Early January 1959 was devoted to March of Dimes activities: a tea at the Governor's Mansion in Des Moines and another at the Ackworth farmhouse. At mid-month, Mrs. Sayre flew to New York for a National Safety Council meeting, and, recalling her pleasure in the London Theatre, attended a Broadway performance of *The Dark at the Top of the Stairs*.

A meeting of the President's Committee for Traffic Safety at the White House made Washington, D.C., her next stop, and here she took time to help Alice look for a house, have dinner with the Roger Flemings, attend an antique show, and lunch with friends.

More pleasure was now combined with the business on Ruth Sayre's agenda. In February she had a brief respite from Iowa winter in Florida, visiting Sarasota, Naples, Key West, Miami, and Palm Beach. Later that month she returned to Washington to see that Alice was settled into her new home in Arlington.

In the years of Mrs. Sayre's heaviest organizational responsibilities, women like Alice and Edith Smith of Ackworth had provided household help, and they were regarded as fond friends rather than employees. Mrs. Sayre's good fortune in finding the assistance she needed continued, but at sixty-three, she had the vigor to wash, iron, and clean "all the books and bookcases" herself.

One new experience of 1959 was a beauty salon manicure, and there was time to note (as Ruth Sayre did March 11), "Saw crescent moon with Venus at upper point—comes once in ten years."

As always, she was working on ACWW resolutions, and she attended a CWC meeting in Kansas City March 17 and 18. Later that month, she went to Des Moines for "a plane ticket and two hats" for an Easter holiday with Alice in New York.

At the Summer Conference of the Farm Bureau women, Ruth Sayre recalled the first of such conferences in wartime "held at the Iowa State Fairgrounds in the Women's Building. We ate in the old 4-H dining hall and slept in 4-H dorms. A few roamed the place most of the night whispering and laughing. Even though we were in the midst of a deadly serious and tragic war, there was some time for fun. It was a step up in the world to hold our meetings in the hotel and have dinner in Younker's Tea Room, and at the suggestion of V. B. Hamilton, secretary-treasurer of the Iowa Farm Bureau, there was a red rose at every woman's place at the table."

A June meeting of the Farm Film Foundation in Washington was followed by a meeting of the Women's Advisory Council in the Black Hills, and then Ruth Sayre went home to prepare for summer visitors—Helen's Cindy and Martha Scott.

On July 30 Ruth Sayre and Cindy flew to New York, where Alice met them and Cindy took another flight to Boston. With one free day in New York before her departure for the Triennial in Scotland, Mrs. Sayre visited the Soviet Exhibit and saw *Anatomy of a Murder.*

Arriving in Glasgow August 2, she proceeded to Edinburgh to meet the United States delegation of 180 women. Attendance was better than it had been in Ceylon, and the constituent societies had had time to study the Survey Report and send in their resolutions. Thus the report was implemented, and Gerda Van Beekhoff, the new president, said, "ACWW has greatly benefited from Mrs. Sayre's outstanding leadership. She said, 'Are we to be an organization for action in the international field, or are we to be a clearing house for discussion?' And the answer is, 'An organization for *action!*' Ruth Sayre has seen the light and passed it on in her own special and warm way. I am convinced that the moment of her becoming ACWW's president was essential to ACWW's existence in this world. The new paths that needed to be taken in the postwar years were clearly seen by Ruth Sayre, and it was with the greatest courage and vision that she was leading the way."

Alice Van Wert (who in 1975 married Dr. William Murray, the Iowa State University professor who founded Living History Farms) says, "Another group had been working before the Nairobi Triennial and had sent delegates its survey report, which advocated more centralized administration in London with fewer council meetings and less input by society representatives. I was pleased to find that only a small minority spoke for it in Ceylon."

The minority voice was silenced at Edinburgh, and Mrs. Sayre's long, hard work bore fruit at last in the acceptance of a new pattern of administration for ACWW.

In a report telephoned from Edinburgh, Ruth Sayre said, "High on the list of things to report back home will be the plea of a small, dark, sari-clad Pakistani woman that the conference, 'in the interest of safeguarding the human race from extinction, urge suspension of nuclear tests destructive to humanity.' She said, 'We must make it known that the women of the world are against the nuclear armament race.'

"A Canadian woman opposed the resolution because not all nations are represented in ACWW, notably Russia, and 'if one nation refuses, we have got to have it as a protection, and if bombs are made, they must be tested.'

"The United States delegation abstained from voting—rare for this group—but the resolution was passed. The American women felt that the resolution was involved with diplomacy and decided to remain silent rather than take a stand against the proposal."

Mrs. Sayre also spoke of the $25,000 a year raised by United States farm women for the Pennies-for-Friendship fund, their correspondence with Letter Friends in other countries, and their welcome to foreign visitors.

She noted that women of Ghana and Malaya joined the conference officially for the first time and that interested observers were sent by Nepal, Japan, British Guiana, Greece, and Sierra Leone. The ACWW was now some six million women strong.

Following the conference, the American women visited in Scottish homes, and Ruth Sayre felt a particularly strong tie to Grandpa McLaughlin's heritage as she visited Aberdeen, Inverness, and Ft. William.

Mrs. Sayre always had known how to make good use of a plane ticket, and at the end of the Scottish sojourn, she flew to Munich to visit John and Barbara.

Together, they saw the sights, and Mrs. Sayre thought it ironic that Hitler, who created the ugly destruction she had seen in 1948 and 1949, could have been sensitive to the beauty of Berchtesgaden.

They went to Salzburg and Garmisch, and at Dachau, Ruth Sayre felt the heavy pall of past evil. She turned with relief to the good food, good music, and beautiful art and architecture in the Germany that had outlived Hitler.

On September 17 John had an "alert" to report for duty. He took his mother to the airport for a flight to Spain, where she visited Madrid and Granada and said of the Don Quixote country near La Mancha, "There are hills and mountains and whitewashed villages—new towns where land has been redistributed. They grow grapes, wheat, and olives."

She visited Cordoba, and in Seville she was sick enough to call for a physician and stay in bed for nearly two days. Returning to Madrid, she felt well enough to resume her enthusiastic sight-seeing, first in Toledo and then in Lisbon, Portugal.

Mrs. Sayre expected to be in Washington for a Monday Civil Defense meeting, but the plane was delayed, and she did not complete the thirteen-hour flight until 2 a.m. on Thursday. Having missed several meetings by this time, she rested for a day and then attacked the tasks of shopping, making curtains, and painting the bedroom of Alice's house. She regarded the rainy afternoon she spent putting a jigsaw puzzle together as playing hookey.

From Washington she flew to Chicago for a National Safety Council meeting, and then she was at home for nearly a week before going to Kansas City for the CWC annual meeting. She had been away for nearly three months, but without Raymond to come home to, what did it matter? Unlike many mothers, she could and would go to her children wherever they were.

Reviewing the old year and looking forward to 1960, Ruth Sayre was startled to realize that she had been passionately involved with

ACWW for three decades and that she soon would be sixty-four. The years without her parents, Raymond, Helen, and many friends had seemed long, but the others had melted like April snow.

In the second week of the new year, she flew to Lansing, Michigan, for a seminar and then to Washington, where she met with President Eisenhower and the Committee for Traffic Safety in the Oval Office of the White House. She remained in Washington long enough to see that all was well with Alice and to attend a performance of *Mary Stuart* at the National Theater before flying to Berkeley for a safety seminar.

A day in San Francisco was followed by a stop in Los Angeles and a ten-day visit with her cousin, Grace Cooper Hardy, which included trips to Disneyland, the antique shops of Glendale, Palm Springs (where President Eisenhower was playing golf), Beverly Hills, Santa Monica, and Pasadena.

Mrs. Sayre returned to Ackworth in time for a February 8 meeting of her BPW club, but after a two-day Iowa snowstorm, she decided to precede a late February safety seminar in Atlanta with a visit to Florida: Tampa, St. Augustine, Cape Canaveral, and Palm Beach.

Visiting Alice in Arlington in early March, Mrs. Sayre went to the theater, saw some films, and made a brief trip to New York before resuming committee meetings in the capital.

For years Ruth Sayre had been too busy to be a baby-sitting grandmother, but now she had the pleasure of keeping five-year-old Mary Alice for a day or going to the home of Bill and Ruthann to stay with all the children for several days in late March.

The early days of April were spent in meetings in New York, but Mrs. Sayre couldn't wait to get home to her yard work, which she attacked energetically for a full week.

John was being discharged from the army, and the news that he and Barbara were coming home from Germany fired his mother with the zeal to clean closets, the basement, and the silver while another woman did the heavy cleaning. Alice was coming home too, and all the children would be present for the recognition dinner planned by the Warren County Farm Bureau for April 27 at Simpson College to honor Ruth Buxton Sayre.

It was a grand and glorious affair with 300 guests. The theme, "From Model T to Jet and Going Yet," was tailor-made for the woman the London *Evening Standard* had called "Round-the-World Momma."

President Eisenhower wired greetings, as did the Rt. Rev. Msgr. L. G. Ligutti in the Vatican, William Randolph Hearst, and many others. Testimonials were offered by L. J. Nickle, former Warren County agent; Louise Rosenfeld; V. B. Hamilton; Alice Van Wert; J. William

*The Warren County Farm Bureau's 1960
recognition dinner for Ruth Sayre prompted this
family portrait: Ruthann and Bill; Mrs.
Sayre; Alice; Barbara and John; and Bill
and Ruthann's children, William R., Ann J.,
and Mary A.*

Bethea, executive secretary of the President's Committee on Traffic Safety; Mrs. Everett Spangler, chairman of the Country Women's Council; and Roger Fleming.

Allan Kline delivered the main address, noting, "It is a brutal fact of life that we cannot continue to improve the health conditions which result in a longer life span unless we also keep births and deaths in balance. It will inevitably end in violence such as the world has never before seen, possibly within the next twenty-five years."

Kline pointed out that the long continued increase of inflation in the United States was inconsistent with our capitalistic theory and said that curtailing the power of labor leaders would do nothing to solve the labor problem. The difficulty was in restraining the power of labor unions. Proceeding to the heart of the matter, agriculture, Kline admitted that agricultural problems might be solved by government controls, but he doubted if such a solution was in line with the American system.

John and Barbara had returned to Ackworth on the very day of the dinner, Alice had arrived, and Bill was present with his family, of course, being partner and neighbor as well as the son of the honoree. Ruth Sayre posed with her children for a photograph in which they all admired an album of pictures from her busy past presented at the dinner. Bill's children were all dressed up for Grandma's big evening and were much admired by the guests.

Commenting on the event in the *Indianola Record-Herald*, publisher Lewis S. Kimer wrote, "This week we feel entirely inadequate in putting together a few words which might, in some small way, portray the contribution of Mrs. Raymond Sayre. She not only was honored this week by her community, but by her friends and admirers all over the world. Mrs. Sayre has left her mark completely around the world from the address, Ackworth, Iowa. It never occurred to this farm woman that she needed an ivory tower or a Park Avenue apartment to sell an ideal in which she so firmly believed. She is proud of her Ackworth address in Warren County, and that probably describes Mrs. Sayre and her success better than anything we might say.

"A firm believer in democracy, she has attempted to lift people, not only in her own community, but everywhere the sun shines, by pointing out to them how they can help themselves. By so doing, she has left the flavor of the true American democracy wherever she has been. . . . We salute her and hope that she continues to go until the jet is placed in the vintage the Model T finds itself today."

The glow of the recognition dinner and its aftermath prompted Ruth Sayre to sort her papers, all carefully kept, between a safety meeting in Evanston, gardening, Ladies' Aid, pouring at the Simpson College commencement tea, and proudly attending Ann's dance recital.

The text of a radio talk by R. K. Bliss, Director of Extension at Iowa State University, was sent to her in May, and it read, "Like most prominent people, Mrs. Sayre started her public career in a small community and then progressed to larger activities. Mrs. Sayre believed strongly in farm organization as an effective method in improving agricultural conditions and also believed women should have a more active part in it."

Bliss spoke of her active support of education and her close cooperation with Neale S. Knowles of the Extension Service and added,

"Mrs. Sayre apparently had something in leadership which can be explained only in moral and spiritual terms. She always stood for high moral standards. People instinctively believed in her and cooperated with her. These were qualities that endeared her to Iowa and later to others in her wide spheres of activity."

Resting a bit on her laurels, Ruth Sayre was braiding rugs for John and Barbara, who now lived in Des Moines, whenever she had a few moments, and on a Wednesday in June she spent the day reading John Galbraith's *The Affluent Society* after having a tooth pulled. The next day, however, she washed, ironed, mended, and sorted a box of papers from the basement.

After the Farm Bureau summer conference, she started to decipher Grandpa Buxton's diary and spent many happy hours reliving his experiences.

Trips to San Francisco and Washington in July were followed by an August trip to the East with Billy and Ann to pick up Alice for an auto tour of New England and Canada. She noted in her date book, "Children good." After that holiday—a week in New York and another in Washington—going through the mail at Ackworth was a two-day job.

The presidential election year involved Ruth Sayre as state chairman for the Women for Nixon-Lodge, a group that met every Friday, and she also served with the Nixon Volunteers in Iowa.

In October Gerda Van Beekhoff was Mrs. Sayre's guest in Ackworth while attending the annual CWC meeting in Des Moines. The Dutch president of ACWW said, "I have borrowed Ruth's sayings, always giving her credit. 'The windows on the world through ACWW,' 'Building bridges of friendship in ACWW,' and, speaking of the membership, 'Out of our diversity can come strength if we work together to get agreement and harmony on the things that we can.' Another favorite of mine is, 'For what will it profit a woman to be wise in the skill of bottling food and adept in the arts and crafts if she lacks knowledge and understanding of the world in which she lives and of the forces that make her world what it is?' I use that when encouraging members to be alert on the things and events surrounding them."

In Washington with Alice in December, Mrs. Sayre attended meetings of the President's Committee on Traffic Safety and addressed her Christmas cards, a three-day project, before going home to Ackworth for the holiday. Alice soon followed, and for the first time in several years, Ruth Sayre could write in her datebook square for December 25, "All family here for the day."

22

Member of Honor

IN 1961, when few Americans had yet perceived the turbulence of the new decade, Ruth Buxton Sayre sensed it and responded with a more determined ordering of her own sphere. She had reached sixty-five, the age of retirement for many, but she continued her existing responsibilities and took on new ones.

She flew to Washington and Chicago repeatedly on National Safety Council business, participated in CWC revision meetings, served on the Cancer Society board, and accepted the state rural chairmanship of the Iowa Heart Association.

Happy times with the family and with old friends of the Pi Phi Alumnae Club, the Thimble Club, the Older Youth Group, and the Ackworth Garden Club filled other days—almost. The busiest schedule could not banish the occasional moment of anomie, the staring off into space with the thought that Raymond had been gone for seven years, Helen for four.

In her youth and middle years, Raymond's presence and support had lent joy to Ruth's efforts. Now, duty and habit made it possible for her to go on, but Raymond still seemed very near as she led the traditional vespers at the AFBF annual convention in Chicago and as she prepared both dinner and supper for nineteen on Christmas Day.

Ruth Sayre often reflected that her heaviest responsibilities seemed to stop just when she needed them most. She was free to go to the 1962 ACWW Triennial in Melbourne, Australia, but she was not needed there in an official capacity, and she would be raking leaves at the Ackworth farm during the excitement of the international gathering.

Any sense of exclusion that Mrs. Sayre might have felt was banished on Saturday, October 27, when she received the news that she had been named Member of Honor, a distinction created at the 1947 Amsterdam Triennial, where she assumed the ACWW presidency. This recognition of outstanding service to ACWW entitled her to vote in any conference meeting and to attend any meetings of the ACWW Council. If she had had any notion of a deferential stepping aside, the citation wiped it out.

Ruth Buxton Sayre was the first American Member of Honor in the history of the organization, and Alice Van Wert, then chairman of the Iowa Farm Bureau Women, said, "In my mind, she is without question the most deserving person in the ACWW realm for this honor. I have seen her work so very hard and experience both joy and sorrow as her reward, so no one is more pleased than I to see her receive this award.

"Again and again she emphasized as she talked to European and Asian women, 'Women should not do heavy work on farms (they don't in America), for one of the best contributions a farmer's wife can make is in the service to the home and community.'

"She challenged women to use their organizations and individual influences to build democracy. She said, 'When I hear women complaining of the mess men made of the world, I remind them that women have the power to mold the minds of men.' "

Presiding at the Melbourne Triennial, Gerda Van Beekhoff was delighted to accord her mentor the highest tribute ACWW could pay to a country woman.

The honorary lifetime membership crowned Ruth Sayre's year, as did the fact that the Survey Report finally was to be put into effect and a letter from Eleanor Roberts written during the Triennial, "How we miss you here! The conference is not the same without you!"

In the summer of 1963 Ruth Sayre spent three weeks in South America with a BPW group following the annual convention of the American Business and Professional Women in Miami. She was bent on involving Central and South American women in ACWW as she traveled through Venezuela, Trinidad, Brazil, Argentina, Uruguay, Chile, Peru, and Panama.

Her observations included, "Corruption in government there is accepted as a normal thing, and until they get out of this way of thinking and put more emphasis on their responsibility to the people, they will continue to have serious problems."

In Brazil she found inflation to be a great difficulty, and poverty was widespread.

"Our hosts in Argentina had a great time trying to figure out what to call me as a farm lady," she said, "so they called me a rancher."

She visited with Herb Howell of Iowa State University, who was in Peru to assist the government with land reform, and he told her that seventy-five percent of the land was in the hands of five percent of the people.

"Of course when you divide land, you get reduced production," she said. "One of the studies being made is to see how large a farm should be so as not to reduce production. They just aren't producing enough to feed their people, as their population is increasing faster than that of any country in the world.

"The migration of the poor people to the cities has grave political implications because, when they get to the city, they live in slums with no jobs, not enough to eat, and become the prey of agitators.

"I was trying to find new members for ACWW," she confessed with a smile, "and eventually, Iowa Farm Bureau Women brought a Brazilian woman to this country for a visit. Later, Brazil joined."

Following the South American trip, Ruth Sayre told of her experiences at the annual meeting of the Country Women's Council in Madison, Wisconsin, and in November she was named Woman of the Year at the sixteenth annual Business and Professional Women's Bosses' Dinner in Iowa.

The year 1964 would bring radical changes in Mrs. Sayre's life. After months of deliberation, her son Bill and his wife Ruthann had reached a decision to leave the farm. Bill would accept a position with the Continental Illinois National Bank and Trust Company as a real estate officer and farm property manager in January, and Ruthann and the children would move to Wilmette, Illinois, to join him when school was out.

The farming partnership started seventeen years earlier by Ruth and Raymond Sayre and their son would continue, but in a different manner. Bill's management expertise would be utilized, and Ruth Sayre would become more intimately involved with the farming operation, assuming the duties of keeping the farm records and receiving and disbursing all funds.

The school girl who wanted to abolish mathematics had become the woman who worked successfully with the figures of a substantial farm operation, and because she had learned economics on the firing line, she knew what it was all about.

In late May 1964 Ruth Sayre was elected to the Simpson College Board of Trustees, which gave her a satisfying sense of continuity. Her grandfather, her father, and her husband had preceded her on the board.

Ruthann and the children moved during the third week of June, disrupting that deep feeling of continuity. It seemed strange to Mrs.

Sayre to look to the northwest and know that the house where so many glad memories had been made was empty. When the banker's daughter broke from her mold to become a farm wife, there must have been a glimmer of intention to lay the foundation for generations of life on the land in line with Raymond's dream, but this was not to be the case in her own family. But who can say how much Ruth Sayre's life and thought encouraged other farm families to hang on for future generations? And perhaps Bill Sayre was of infinitely greater help to farmers in his Chicago bank than he could have been had he remained on the land.

The added responsibility of the day-to-day operation of the farm did not prevent Mrs. Sayre from subjecting the affairs of the nation and the world to rigorous examination. The October 1964 issue of the *Farm Journal* carried her article, "Who's Been Doing Your Thinking Lately?''—a repudiation of the charge of apathy on the part of the American public, women in particular.

"Now I resent this," she wrote, "for I *do* care, a great deal, about my government, about what happens to my country. . . . Then what is my trouble as a citizen? Well, for one thing, I think I'm expected to make decisions on issues about which I don't have enough facts. Many of you doubtless feel the same way."

She told how she had sat in on a round-table discussion of peace and was told by the leader how many missiles the United States had compared with the USSR. She said, "Emotionally, it could have been fairly easy to agree that we must all disarm, as he urged, in order to save the world. But I do read a good deal about world affairs now that I have more time to myself than I once had." And, she continued, she had read enough to be suspicious of the leader's facts.

Clear-headed as always, Ruth Sayre perceived that the group was being pressured by fears and emotions, not by realities. She said, "Fear is an unstable prop on which to rest our decisions. (The things we fear may turn out to be not threats, but blessings. Rural Free Delivery began in 1896 despite cries that it would bankrupt the country. County agents, in the early days, were often distrusted.)"

She warned against slogans that oversimplify problems and said, "One of the easiest ways is to listen only to one side of an argument or question and close our minds to any other viewpoint. This makes us feel comfortable, less upset. Of course, it may lead to inaccurate conclusions. And it means that we are letting somebody else do our thinking for us."

Observing that even farm families, the most individualistic of creatures, seemed to want more and more to conform, Mrs. Sayre admitted that conformity was usually the way to popularity, but she urged her readers to exercise an inquiring mind that looks for the whole truth beyond too-pat answers to difficult problems.

"This involves getting all the facts we can from reading and from listening to a variety of material. It also involves critical judging and evaluating of all we read and hear. It means asking questions like 'Who said it?' 'What do these spokesmen represent?' If I read it on the editorial page, 'What is the philosophy or slant of the publication? The background of the writer? The point of view?' "

She suggested, "To make intelligent decisions, I think it helps me to ask myself, 'What am I for?' Not just 'What am I against?' "

She wrote of loyalty to an organization, saying, "When it's time to reach a group decision for action, majority opinion must, of course, prevail. If the organization's stand is repugnant to you, you'll have to decide whether to get out of the group or stay in and make your influence felt." She herself had taken both courses of action.

Finally, she wrote, "I must question my own motives. How much of my own self-interest is involved in what I think? The fact that I live on the farm makes me look at things quite differently from the city person."

Quoting Margaret Mead, she wrote, " 'Human beings have remained human because there were women whose duty it was to provide continuity to their lives . . . to ease pain . . . to sympathize . . . to listen . . . to soothe and support and sustain and stimulate. . . .'

"But our womanly emotions do interfere sometimes with our being objective and effective citizens or organization members or officers. If we don't think for ourselves, we only parrot someone else's opinions—may even parrot someone else's words.

"To be the individual persons we were intended to be, we have to grind facts through our own brains and think things out. Then we can strike a balance between reason and emotion. Then we can be fair and not rigid. Then our beliefs will be our own and will be sincere. Then we will be creditable citizens and truly serve our country."

Ruth Buxton Sayre not only said these things, she meant them, and she did what she said.

23

A Signal from the Heart

AT the ACWW Triennial in Dublin in 1965, Mrs. Aroti Dutt of India was elected president, and she writes, "I came into the ACWW orbit after Mrs. Sayre's term as world president was over, but nonetheless, the contribution of her leadership by then had become very much a part of ACWW history.

"I have been helped often by her advice based on sound judgment in many vital matters concerning our work. I remember the poignant moments in Dublin when I was elected president unopposed. I wrote my presidential speech based on my thoughts over a long period, and friends advised me to discard it and give a talk on the spur of the moment. I was vacillating and went to Ruth for guidance. She said, 'You may get much friendly advice, but you are the president. The decision is yours. From today, you have to think as a president of ACWW, the head of a worldwide body.'

"This idea was not new, yet her words came to me at a very special moment, and I always thought of them in my moments of indecision while I held the position."

Mrs. Dutt would visit Ruth Sayre in what she called "her lovely home at Ackworth" in 1966 during an official tour of the United States.

The USSR, a vast country encompassing millions of agricultural acres, held a special fascination for Ruth Sayre, much as she disapproved of its system of government, and besides, she said, "It was one of the few places I hadn't been."

She was granted a visa for a 2,000-mile bus trip through the Soviet

Union, embarking on that journey after the Dublin conference. Wheat fields sweeping to infinity, the bent backs of women in the beet rows and collective farm workers lined up as if for inspection were registered among her observations along with the Faberge treasures and the gowns of the czarinas in the Kremlin Musuem.

As the bus rolled through small villages, she longed to stop and visit with the women in babushkas as she had done with the women of other nations, but this was not permitted.

"I felt stymied," she said, "if only I could have met the people!" As she had proved in India, the language barrier could not bar communication, but in the USSR even smiles and gestures were not readily exchanged. "There were no ACWW members and wouldn't be. Russian women applied for membership but were turned down because their organization didn't make its own policies."

The year 1966 would be a difficult one for Ruth Sayre, but she didn't realize how difficult until the April day when her chest hurt and her work with the Iowa Heart Association gave her a strong clue to the nature of the problem. She telephoned John's wife, Barbara, asking to be taken to the hospital. Fortunately, John and Barbara had moved back to Indianola, and Barbara was at home, so no time was lost.

The eight weeks Ruth Sayre spent in Methodist Hospital, Des Moines, seemed much longer to a woman who had not spent a fraction of that time immobilized in her whole lifetime. Cards and letters from friends all over the world overflowed her bed table, and as soon as John and Barbara took one batch home, new stacks would rise.

As Mrs. Sayre's condition improved, she responded to her well-wishers by donning a hat and sitting up in bed for a photograph captioned, "Ready to go!" The enforced idleness had been as galling as the rope her mother once used to tie her to a tree outside the little yellow house.

During her convalescence, Ruth Sayre was featured in the *Des Moines Register* Women of Iowa series in a piece by Mary Bryson which began, "Almost every possible honor that can be given to a farm woman has been conferred on her. . . . She is surely Iowa's most traveled farm woman, and her bright friendliness and common sense have done a great deal to shape the picture that women of other countries have of American womankind.

"Though she was seventy on her last birthday and is recuperating from a heart attack that hospitalized her for eight weeks, she still raises her gentle voice in behalf of farm women everywhere."

Mary Bryson noted that Mrs. Sayre had just finished writing a history of the Warren County rural schools, was still an active National Safety Council board member, and was vitally involved with the

Associated Country Women of the World and the Iowa Farm Bureau Women. The article ended, "In her many services to the people of Indianola, of Iowa, and of the nations, Mrs. Sayre has earned the respect of her countrymen far and near."

Ruth Sayre had, indeed, earned both respect and love around the globe. She was never casual in relationships, extending herself generously but with an ultimate reserve. In letters to friends of long standing, she signed herself "Mrs. Sayre." Perhaps this private core provided the staying power for lengthy public service.

There is no indication that Mrs. Sayre ever swallowed her own publicity whole, even though she might have been entitled to do so in a time when honest admiration could not be confused with hype. She did, however, know how to accept compliments with grace rather than with the disclaimer that makes the offerer feel foolish.

Released from the hospital with special diet requirements and orders to follow a calmer regimen, Ruth Sayre noted the pronouncements of Lyndon B. Johnson, the second Democratic president with whom she had no mitigating personal contact, with some annoyance. She was particularly piqued when President Johnson and Secretary of Agriculture Orville Freeman suggested that farm prices were causing inflation. Had her efforts to disprove this view in the early fifties been in vain?

Pique with Johnson did not follow party lines that summer. Iowa Governor Harold Hughes, a Democrat, was disappointed that the president preceded a visit to Iowa with a speech in Omaha that took the edge off his appearance in the Hawkeye State and commented, "I feel like a bangle on a horse's tail."

Still under orders to rest, Mrs. Sayre knitted, learned needlepoint, and visited her children and grandchildren while she continued to read and keep up on world affairs. She also maintained her intense involvement with ACWW.

In the fall of 1967, Epsilon Sigma Phi, the Extension Service fraternity at Iowa State University, awarded Mrs. Sayre a Certificate of Recognition to an Iowa Citizen with the following statement: "From organizing farm women in a rural township in Iowa to organizing them on an international scale, Mrs. Raymond Sayre has shown leadership qualities matching the best in public diplomats. But along with this ability, she has maintained a genuine sense of humor, a humility, and a sincerity that have won her the respect and following of those she has encountered—from the 'grass roots' of Iowa to the other side of the globe. Mrs. Sayre has been a strong and active supporter of education. In her early years with the Iowa Farm Bureau Federation, she helped develop the Extension home economics educational program. Since then, her belief in the citizenship responsibilities of farm women has spread around the globe in her contacts through leadership in the Associated Country Women of the World.''

Ruth Sayre attended the ACWW Triennial in East Lansing, Michigan, in 1968, and Stella Bell says, "She was a most valued member of the American Planning Committee. This was a very happy conference planning time for me, as I was once again working closely with Mrs. Sayre, and the other officers of the planning committee were old and dear friends.

"I well remember one night in 1967 during the Country Women's Council held at East Lansing, Michigan, so that meetings of the Planning Committee could be held. After the evening session, Mrs. Sayre, Ruth Miller, Lois Gross, and I retired to one of the bedrooms with our mountain of papers and started to work on Conference plans, sorting out the problems, getting tired, but not wanting to give up, for this was a wonderful chance for us to work together—much easier than working by mail. Around 2 a.m. we paused to make a cup of coffee and realized we were all hungry. Someone had given me a parcel, and Mrs. Sayre said, 'Do you think that gift could be something to eat?' It was— goodies. So like naughty school girls, we had our dormitory feast. Next morning, the dignified, older stateswoman was once again in charge.''

One feature of the East Lansing Triennial brought a touch of sadness to Ruth Sayre. The American delegates had their husbands with them for USA Day, and how she wished that Raymond could have been with her.

Mrs. Dutt presided, saying in her presidential message, "Gather knowledge and friendship when you have the time and opportunity. We find that discord started at home gradually spreads; the frustrations of individual lives spread like wildfire and envelop the whole country and the world.'' She urged the international housekeeping that was so much a part of Ruth Sayre's life.

Mrs. Dutt says, "Ruth had to appear many times before television and press at the Michigan conference, and I was amazed to find how she kept track of ACWW work in detail.''

Dietary restrictions following her heart attack had made Ruth Sayre much thinner, and her hair was snowy white in 1968, but she carried her seventy-two years lightly.

She was proud of Bill when he was elected president of the Chicago Farmers Club in June 1969, and she herself was soon to win awards that would please her as much as seemingly more important honors. At the annual flower show of the Ackworth Garden Club in the Friends Church at Ackworth, she won the Tri-color Award for the best arrangement in the artistic division for an arrangement of Queen Elizabeth tea roses, and she also won in the Fuji class. That long-ago joshing from a thresher about her nasturtium centerpiece had not discouraged her permanently.

Another pursuit of Mrs. Sayre's in 1969 was collecting old books, maps, lunch pails, and other country school artifacts for a one-room schoolhouse the Warren County Historical Society was restoring and maintaining at the Warren County Fairgrounds.

In September 1969 she flew to London for an ACWW Council meeting, ready to work as hard as ever and offer advice when it was sought.

Ruth Sayre's chief concession to the tumultuous sixties was shortening her skirts. Otherwise, she pursued her concerns for country people just as implacably as she had done in the Roaring Twenties.

24

Full Circle

THE 1970s began with a heavy overlay from the previous decade, and Ruth Sayre found much that was good in it, including a concern for human rights and for the ecology. She remained at home in the world because she never became ossified in any time span or suffered the pangs of the generation gap so widely felt throughout the nation.

She had her pleasures, including a Caribbean cruise with two good friends, Mrs. Paul Palmer from Missouri and Mrs. Philip Jones from Florida, and as always, she was more than a tourist, setting her mind to means of improving the lot of women in the countries they visited.

The year 1970 brought its share of adversity, too. A farrowing house at the Ackworth farm caught fire, killing 15 sows and 180 pigs.

Although Mrs. Sayre's affiliation with the Business and Professional Women's Club came late in her life, she embraced it with youthful enthusiasm and was named the Indianola club's Sweetheart at the 1970 annual Employers Appreciation night at the Indianola Country Club.

Ruth Sayre received a standing ovation as an ACWW Member of Honor at the 1971 annual CWC meeting in Kansas City, Missouri. Her speech to the council concerned the development of philosophy, policy, and constitution of ACWW, which she had been reviewing for the purpose of writing a history.

With forty-one years of ACWW experience, she was well qualified to tell the story, and she began, "History is, for most of us, the dullest of subjects—a conglomeration of dates. In this account I will try to

*The year 1971 brought happy times with friends
like this Caribbean cruise with Jean Jones (left)
and Georgia Palmer (right).*

make history come alive for you by relating it to the present scene.'' She
did just that in fifteen concise and vivid pages.

Mrs. Sayre's interest in history closer to home persisted, and in July
1971 the women's meeting of the Warren County Farm Bureau was
held at the fairgrounds. Members met at 10 o'clock in the morning to
clean the fair stand before eating their sack lunches. Then they toured
the Mt. Hope school with a richly informed guide, Ruth Buxton Sayre,
author of the history of the Warren County schools.

The 1971 ACWW Triennial was to be held in Oslo, Norway, in
July, and Mrs. Sayre flew to Europe early to tour Germany and Norway

with Alice, who was working temporarily in Cologne. John and Barbara were vacationing in Europe at the time, and the four Sayres met in Munich.

The chief concern of the Oslo conference was the length of officers' terms. More than half the resolutions and amendments to the constitution sent in by constituent organizations dealt with this question. Put to a vote in committee and in the plenary session, a resolution was passed that no officer of ACWW with the exception of honorary treasurer could hold the same office for more than two terms (six years).

The American delegation believed that a three-year term for world president was "all that any woman should have in these times."

Mrs. Rex Strait of Keosauqua, a voting delegate representing the Iowa Farm Bureau Women, said, "Since this resolution had lost in the committee, Iowa's Mrs. Raymond Sayre, a past world president of ACWW, prepared a minority report on the reasons for having just one three-year term for president, which she presented at plenary. As she does with everything, she had an outstanding presentation, but it lost."

Ruth Sayre was no stranger to losing, and she accepted it philosophically, going on to enjoy the lavish hospitality of the Norwegians before a trip through Denmark, Austria, Italy, the French Riviera, and Switzerland with Mrs. L. C. Shivvers of Knoxville, Iowa.

She would meet with eleven of the Oslo delegates at the Master Farm Homemakers Guild in Cedar Rapids, Iowa, in October to renew memories of the Norwegian conference, which attracted women from forty-eight countries.

In 1972 Mrs. Sayre unveiled a plaque at the dedication of a new dormitory at Simpson College, and this year marked her new status as a great-grandmother. Ruggie (George Ruggles Coolidge III) had married and was the father of a son, Chad.

Also in 1972 Alice was posted to Nigeria, which lured her mother back to Africa. Collecting Nigerian carvings, Ruth Sayre said, "Patterns of culture and attitudes of people in other lands have seemed worthwhile bringing home to add significance and happiness to life. Blue Meissen cups from Germany, chased brass bowls from India, copper trays from Cairo, and now these carvings fit with my American gadgets as if they had always belonged there."

Two years later all of Ruth Sayre's possessions and treasurers would have to find a new place of belonging. In October 1974 she moved from the Ackworth farm to Indianola, and she said, "After forty-six years in the same house, it was quite a decision and quite an undertaking."

John Sayre notes, "Mother wanted to bring everything with her."

This being impossible, Mrs. Sayre chose to absent herself from the dismantling of her longtime home. John and Barbara served as

Ruth Sayre and her brother, William Buxton III,
were present for the 1972 dedication of Buxton
Hall on the Simpson College campus.

overseers during the eight hours required to load the van, and when
that job was finished, they discovered that their own car was blocking
the drive. Furthermore, the keys were missing.

"Family car keys always were kept on the kitchen window sill at
home because different people drove the cars," John says, "and that
training lay so deep that I couldn't remember putting my own car keys
on the sill. Mother could have told me, but she didn't want to be there,
and that was the last place I looked."

Listening to the story, Ruth Sayre smiled and said, "That's what
training does for you!"

The town house on Girard in Indianola is a spacious, split-level home of recent construction, but Mrs. Sayre's antiques and international art objects were very much at home there. Repeating the colors of the Ackworth farmhouse eased the transition, as did the bookcases Mrs. Sayre added immediately.

The house looks out on Buxton Park, given to the city by William Buxton, Sr., in 1906, and Buxton Street is a few blocks away. Across the alley is the Alpha Chi Omega sorority house and a house that once served as the home of Simpson College presidents. Although Ackworth was her home for nearly half a century, returning to Indianola was a matter of coming full circle for Ruth Buxton Sayre.

Important events of 1975 included the marriage of Mrs. Sayre's grandson, Billy, to Carolyn Gwen in Chicago and a ground-breaking ceremony for Simpson's new $2.3 million physical education and recreation center. Ruth Sayre dedicated the sun court adjacent to the indoor pool as Raymond Sayre Court to commemorate her husband's service on the Simpson College Board of Trustees from 1946 until his death in 1954. A smiling Raymond wearing a Simpson letter sweater seemed very near that day, moving Ruth to ponder the myriad varieties of immortality.

The whole nation was in love with memories in 1976, the bicentennial year, and Ruth Sayre rode on the Warren County Farm Bureau float in the Bicentennial parade. She also contributed to the prevailing examination of the past by discussing changes in Iowa farming through the years on Public Television.

On August 26, 1976, Mrs. Sayre was honored by inclusion in the Iowa Women's Hall of Fame along with Susan Glaspell, Pulitzer Prize–winning playwright from Davenport; Agnes Samuelson, Shenandoah educator; and Cora Bussey Hillis, an early child health advocate and civic leader from Des Moines. The ceremony at the Iowa State Fair was sponsored by the Iowa Commission on the Status of Women.

Following a trip to Alaska with Alice in the fall, Mrs. Sayre attended the wedding of Helen's daughter, Cynthia Ann Coolidge, in Sudbury, Massachusetts. Cindy's bridegroom was Marble Mainini.

In 1977 Bill Sayre was elected national president of Alpha Gamma Rho agriculture fraternity. Now vice-president of the nation's seventh largest bank, he was following the banking tradition of the Buxton family.

Always the champion of women's rights, Ruth Sayre moderated the occasional man-hating statements of younger ''sisters'' by remarking quietly, ''I'm the mother of sons, too.'' In 1977 she relived her experience as a college suffragette by leading a parade in support of the Equal Rights Amendment around the Indianola square. This time, she noted sadly, there were no catcalls from Raymond, but there wouldn't

*Ruth Sayre was
the proud grand-
mother of the
bride at the
wedding of Bill
and Ruthann
Sayre's daughter,
Mary Alice, and
Frank Patterson
in June 1977.*

have been had he been alive. He had learned a great deal about
women's rights since that first parade. When the marchers went on to
the State Capitol in Des Moines, the 81-year-old Ruth Sayre stayed in
Indianola.

On June 4, 1977, Mrs. Sayre attended the Wilmette wedding of
Mary Alice, Bill's daughter, and Frank Patterson.

A month later, she was at Living History Farms, an outdoor
museum of agriculture at the west edge of Des Moines conceived by Dr.
William Murray (Alice Van Wert's husband) to accept a Distinguished
Agricultural Award. She received the award, she said, not only for
herself, but for all farm women who wanted to make a better life for
farm families in Iowa.

Ruth Sayre, her white hair incandescent in the sun, was wearing a
hearing aid now, but she laughed about it, saying she guessed she had

inherited deafness from Grandma McLaughlin. What bothered her more was the drastic worsening of her eyesight. She said, "I don't like it very much, but nothing can be done about it."

Her health would not permit attendance at the 1977 ACWW Triennial, but Ruth Sayre's thoughts were in Nairobi, and when Alice Van Wert Murray returned from the African conference, she said, "Even though Mrs. Sayre is no longer able to attend, her influence is strongly felt, and her groundwork prevails. Her favorite line from Plato is remembered by those who have rubbed shoulders with her, 'Those having torches will pass them on to others.' "

And Ruth Sayre carried so many torches. Louise Rosenfeld has seized one to work with the International Educational Services at Iowa State University, developing culture kits for countries all over the world to promote international friendship and understanding.

Who knows how many German women have grasped a passing torch? Gerda Van Beekhoff, a former ACWW world president, visited Germany in the summer of 1977, and she wrote, "Here Mrs. Sayre's visit in 1948 was warmly remembered. Her wisdom and guidance resulted in the acceptance of the German Landfrauen-Verein as a constituent society of ACWW during the Copenhagen conference in 1950. This, too, is gratefully remembered."

Ruth Sayre's old friend, V. B. Hamilton, died on April 8, 1978, in Hampton, Iowa, after a long illness. A few months earlier, he had said of her, "Ruth Sayre is one of the finest women of the world in my time—not the greatest, like Eleanor Roosevelt—but a lady who did wonderful things to help farm people. She has a good sense of humor, and the beautiful thing of it all—that hasn't changed."

Could a person so right for his or her time be born and shaped again? The question prompts another—what created the person Ruth Buxton Sayre became? Was it the Buxtons and the McLaughlins with their staunch English and Scottish genes? Was it Methodism with its "strangely warmed" heart and practical activism? Was it Simpson College with its high ideals and a maverick professor who seemed "pretty pink" for his day? Was it the love of a good man, Raymond Sayre? Was it the Farm Bureau with its paradoxical freedom and strength through numbers? Was it the state of Iowa, at once skeptical and ingenuous; reserved and spontaneous; conservative and innovative? Surely it was all of these and more, and they will never be combined identically again. More's the pity, and yet Ruth Sayre would be the first to say that other men and women will meet their moments, grasping the torch to go on.

On a beautiful May afternoon in 1978 with John at the wheel of the green car she could no longer see well enough to drive, Ruth Sayre returned to Ackworth for a nostalgic look at what was left of the white board fence around the farmstead, the South River vista, the Friends Church, the school with attached playroom, and the post office where Opal Swarthout held sway. Passing the former home of Bill and Ruthann, she pointed out the pasture where Raymond was struck by the falling tree, and she lapsed into a thoughtful silence.

White hair contrasting dramatically with a cardinal red sweater, Ruth Buxton Sayre had a special kind of beauty in spite of the lingering effects of an attack of shingles that had hospitalized her in April. She had endured.

Then she spoke of depending on others for her perceptions of world events, saying, "I have to keep up on things, even though nothing depends on me anymore. You can't change."

Strange words from a woman who has been an outstanding agent of change. Not only has she experienced radical changes in technology and attitudes in her lifetime, but she has run toward the future with hope, persuading others to come along.

In cold print, her persuasions may look too solemn and lofty to act upon, but it must be remembered that Ruth Sayre's innate good humor flowed beneath them like an underground stream, making her much more than a cold crusader.

On the drive home that May afternoon, she pointed out the former dwelling of an Indianola woman who sang at her own funeral by means of a recording, "getting the last word," and that wonderful, rich laughter bubbled forth—the laughter that carried Ruth Buxton Sayre through a full, demanding, and productive life and made her the indomitable first lady of the farm.

INDEX

DATE	ISSUED TO